The

Journey

To Improved Business Performance

by

Stephen J. Thomas

Foreword by Bob Harrell
Chairman and CEO, Management Controls, Inc.

Library of Congress Cataloging-in-Publication Data

Thomas, Stephen J.
  The journey : improving business performance / Steve Thomas.
    p. cm.
  ISBN-13: 978-0-8311-3363-4 (softcover) 1. Organizational
change--Management. 2. Production management. 3. Industrial manage-
ment.
I. Title.
  HD58.8.T488 2008
  658.4'06--dc22

                                    200704736

Industrial Press, Inc.
989 Avenue of the Americas
New York, NY 10018

First Edition, 2008

Sponsoring Editor: John Carleo
Interior Text and Cover Design Photo: Janet Romano
Back Cover Photo: Larry D. Jarvis
Developmental Editor: Robert Weinstein

10 9 8 7 6 5 4 3 2 1

DEDICATION

To my wife
Susan

To my children
Allie
Isabel
Jen
Michael
Peter
Scott

And to my grandchildren
Jacob
Jonah

Author's Note

The books that I have written before *The Journey* were all focused on maintenance and reliability in a plant work environment. Over the years, as I have further developed and presented my material, I have learned that my materials go far beyond their original purpose. In fact, the cultural and soft skill change concepts and techniques apply to all businesses at the level where "the rubber meets the road."

This book is a fictional account about business change made in a plant environment. However, you will quickly see that the concepts apply everywhere. People like Allen Peters, Doug McDonald, Mike Kane, and Todd Bradley exist in every industry and in every business. It should be an easy task for you to take the concepts presented in this story and apply them to change efforts within your business. As you travel on your own journey through this book, ask yourself, "How can I apply the concepts that Todd has learned to my situation?" The answers are there.

Enjoy the story. More important, apply what you learned and help your company reap the benefits.

Steve Thomas

 **TABLE OF CONTENTS**

FOREWORD

How can management be so stuck in their ways as to nearly derail a perfectly good business? Steve Thomas, the author of The Journey, vividly writes of the personalities and actions taken by managers seemingly hell-bent on scuttling a viable enterprise. Fortunately for us, the hero of the story rescues the company using perseverance, technology and hard work. Each reader will take away his or her own lessons from The Journey. What a great way to learn; not by jeopardizing our careers or companies but by following the example of Todd Bradley from failure to success.

We've all been around or worked for bosses that don't get it, don't like us, or both. Each of us at one time or another has felt like leaping across the desk and throttling the person we report to. It may be that some or all of us have been the subject of co-workers' ardent desires to jump over our desk. The point here is that we are each confident that our way is the right way. One good measure of the validity of our position is how much has our way has changed in the last year or two.

Doug McDonald and Mike Kane, as you will read, are both senior managers in their company – each reporting to the Founder and President. They haven't changed their management practices in decades. It's their way or the highway. Our hero, Todd Bradley, knows what to change and how it should be changed. Here's the rub, he threatens his bosses; his technical knowledge conflicts with their "old way". Sound familiar?

I happen to work in a software company. As one of the age-challenged guys here, it is always on my mind that I'm often the sea anchor on this boat. It's not unusual for the folks I work with to look at me with that strange look that says "you really don't get it, do you?" In fact, it's often the case that I don't get it. Unlike Doug and Mike, the anti-heroes of the first few chapters, change for me is not bad, it's good. It's often difficult for me to say, not for the first time, "Run that by me one more time". It may be repetitive and may slow progress but there are no steely grips on my throat. I'm open to change.

While the differences may outweigh the similarities, manufacturing software and manufacturing tangible products share a reliance on people and processes. Reliability (keep the line running) is Todd Bradley's prime objective. His bosses don't get it and Todd Bradley is seemingly helpless to impose a better way. It takes a stroke of bad fortune to open the door to change. Todd steps through the door. He instills a sense of respect for the people he works with and installs a system of repeatable maintenance and operations processes that save the company.

Why is it so tough for enterprises here and around the globe to adapt to new ways? Fundamentally we don't trust change. It represents the risk of failure even when what we've done for decades is crumbling around us. The familiar is better that the unknown. Let's keep on keeping on regardless of the results. Prime examples? High labor content/low value manufacturing – toys, electronics - and high volume/repetitive administrative processes – accounts payable and check processing.

As a nation we didn't change so we've lost most of these businesses. New providers with new ways moved those businesses to their backyard. This almost happens to Todd Bradley's company. Fortunately, Todd knows a better way.

Thousand of jobs and families benefit from Todd's knowledge, persistence and a stroke of luck. Your company can benefit. In fact, it's not difficult. Be open to change, insist on repeatable plant maintenance and operations practices and do what your Mom taught you: be nice to everyone.

It is my pleasure to call Steve Thomas a good friend. Steve talks the talk and walks the walk. I've seen him do so.

I hope you enjoy The Journey as much as I have.

Bob Harrell
Chairman and CEO
Management Controls, Inc.

ACKNOWLEDGEMENTS

I would like to acknowledge John Carleo and Patrick Hansard of Industrial Press Inc. They are more to me than just representatives of the publisher. They have been great advisors and supporters for my work and my ideas, as well as good friends.

I would also like to thank Janet Romano of Industrial Press for her creativity in always coming up with a truly great cover. This time was especially true since she took the cover photo. She is also the person who takes my Word documents and artwork and assembles them into an excellently formatted book.

My thanks are also extended Robert Weinstein, my editor. Robert is the person who takes my writing and fixes the problems so that you the reader can enjoy the content. He has a wonderful knack for fixing things but never altering the concepts or ideas in the text.

I also would like to recognize my good friend Larry Jarvis. I had seen Larry's photography when we worked together and admired his ability and creativity. I appreciate the time and effort he spent in order to take photos of roads in California; one of which became the rear cover of this book.

I want to also thank my son Peter. He invented the concept of TAN as I was driving him back to the train so he could return home to New York City. TAN plays an important role in the book and exists thanks to Peter.

Last, but certainly not least, my sincere thanks to the many very busy people listed on the next page who accepted my request to review and comment on my book before its publication:

Ken Bass
Steve Beamer
Eric Bevevino
Ralph Blanchard
Gerry Bleau
Heinz Bloch
Rob Bloomquist
Dane Brooks
Tom Byerly
Joe Carolan
Paul Casto
Larry Covino
Dick DeFazio
Michael Desabris
Butch DiMezzo
Robert DiStefano
Henry Ellmann
Timothy Goshert
Ramesh Gulati
Todd Gunderson
Bob Harrell
Bruce Hawkins
Charles Hoban
Dr. Melina Hodkiewicz
Eric Huston
Marty Jacobsen
Ken Johnson

Dave Krings
Joel Levitt
Scott McWilliams
Jack R. Nicholas, Jr.
Terry O'Hanlon
Jim Oldach
Dennis Patrick
S. Bradley Peterson
Graeme Poole
Ken Pustizzi
James Reyes-Picknell
John Senior
David Sherwin
Jeff Shuler
Arne Skaalure
Adrian Slywotski
Rusty Smith
Michael Sondalini
Kevin Stewart
Scott Thompson
Michael Turek
Helen Upton-Leis
Henk van Vugt
John Vanier
Louis Volschenk
Todd White
Terry Wireman

WELCOME TO MY WORLD

My day began like all of the others had begun for the last five years. My alarm went off. My dog Paws recognized that not only was it time for me to get up for work, but it was his breakfast time as well. No matter that it was 4:30 in the morning; it was simply the beginning of another day for both of us. The good news for Paws was that following his breakfast he got to go back to sleep. I on the other hand got to go to work. Paws got the better deal.

It's not that I didn't like my job. It just happened to be frustrating and I found that I seemed to like it less and less as time went by. I worked at a plant with really good, knowledgeable, and dedicated people. Having worked with them for five years, I knew they had the best interests of the company at heart. The problem is that we couldn't keep the equipment running. The frequent breakdowns led us to excessive downtime, lost production, and even more recently lost customers. Many people suggested ideas to help correct the problems we experienced, I among them. All were dismissed as impractical, as things that had been tried and failed in the past, or simply not in line with company or plant policy. I had not been able to figure out how running a reliable plant could be against company policy, but Doug McDonald told me this in a roundabout way on more than one occasion. This usually happened as he was dismissing an idea that I shared for his consideration.

Another thing I could never understand was him repeatedly telling me to "just fix what's broken, don't get fancy with your unworkable reliability ideas." This behavior from a plant manager didn't make sense. You would think that he would want to improve the operation.

The other comment that really got me angry was, "if you had fixed it right the first time we wouldn't be having these problems." For some reason he must have thought that my team tried to fix things incorrectly. Fat chance! I had people who had taken it upon themselves to try to make reliability-based repairs. The reason why I say that they had taken it upon themselves is because if Doug had found out, it could have cost them their jobs.

For some reason reliability isn't a word he liked to hear.

I guess you can tell that I harbored a very high level of frustration as I watched our equipment break down and contracts that we should have won wind up in the hands of our competition.

But I am getting a bit ahead of myself. I need to stop a moment and provide you with some background information so that you will understand my company, the work that I do, and the problems we are encountering. Like I said, Paws got the better deal!

My name is Todd Bradley and I work for the American Tractium Company. That's ATPCo, called A–tip–co, for short. We manufacture a product called tractium. You probably have never heard of this material before, but if you look closely on the packaging labels of many items you use in your home, you will find tractium as a key component. There is also one other very important aspect of tractium. It is derived from scrap metal. Strange, but true! Tractium is created by putting scrap metal through a very sophisticated manufacturing process that converts it into tractium.

There are four different types of tractium. Depending on their degree of purity, they can be used in various types of manufactured goods. They are universally called Alpha, Beta, Cappa, and Delta throughout the industry. Once the scrap has been converted, the tractium is then shipped to finished goods manufacturers where it is incorporated into the products that they make. Not only is tractium a valuable additive to increase the life of many of your household products, it is also a very cost-efficient way to recycle scrap.

The company was founded twenty-five years ago by Allen Peters who still is the president and CEO of the company. The initial years for the company were very difficult. The finished goods manufacturers just didn't believe you could take scrap metal and produce an unheard of material, tractium, which could be used to vastly increase the durability of their products. It wasn't until Allen convinced a major manufacturer to use tractium that it gained a foothold in the industry. The risk taken by that manufacturer (who I won't name) made them a fortune. Along with their success came the long-term success of ATPCo.

It took Allen years to get the firm on a solid footing. The capital required for the equipment necessary to produce tractium was very costly and much was still in the developmental stages. This was the bad news. The good news, however, was that the high capital investment for the equipment initially kept others out of the business. Once the process was proven successful, other firms tried to enter the market, but by that time ATPCo was the major player in the United States and some small markets abroad. That is not to say that we don't have competition, but the competitors are limited to a few companies who have the capital and interest in the investment.

That was ATPCo's beginning. The original plant grew and so did the demand for tractium. Over the next ten years, ATPCo built four additional plants in strategic geographical locations. These new plants enabled ATPCo to service the entire U.S. market without any significant shipping costs. These plants were located in the West (the original site), the North, the East, the South, and the exact center of the country. Allen gave them very original names: the Western, Northern, Southern, Eastern and Central plants! Each of the plants was virtually self sufficient. Furthermore, each had four tractium lines so that they could process all four products at the same time. They were also designed so that they could be switched over to run a different tractium product with minimal downtime. Allen was so fanatical about a standard plan for the plants that not only was the equipment identical but so was everything else as well.

Allen's philosophy for operating the original plant and all those that followed was based on his original market practices. At the beginning of the business, the objective was to get tractium out the plant door and into the hands of the customer as quickly as possible. At that time, before tractium was widely accepted as an additive to finished goods, Allen's fear was that if the product didn't get to the market on time, then the demand would evaporate, putting ATPCo out of business.

The result of Allen's fear was the evolution of a set of business values related to production which stated that you needed to run the equipment as hard as required to meet demand. If something broke down along the way, then you needed to fix it as fast as you were able and get back into production. Allen operated the plants in this fashion and his key employees followed his lead. Some of these people were the ones that eventually became his plant managers. My current boss Doug McDonald was one of these people.

The "break it – fix it" mode of operation worked satisfactorily in the beginning because the equipment was new. However, running equipment in this manner over a long period of time began to have serious negative effects on ATPCo. The equipment started to break down more and more frequently. Yes, it was true that the maintenance organization, all of whom were skilled in rapid repair, were able to get the tractium lines running in short order. But the frequency of failure grew. The company's management team never stopped to consider that this mode of operation was no longer required nor applicable. Tractium was "here to stay" and a continuous supply to meet the demand was far better than one interrupted by line shutdowns and equipment failures.

It was around this time of increasing equipment failures, lost production, and high downtime that I was hired at the Western Plant as maintenance manager. I was recruited from another company where I had been able to introduce some preventive maintenance strategies that improved overall performance. Allen found me at a maintenance seminar. I had just completed a presentation on reliability, describing for the audience the work that I and my team had accomplished. Allen and I discussed my talk and work strategy over drinks. Then, following a job interview at ATPCo's corporate office and a great deal of coaxing, I agreed to join the company.

I didn't realize what I was getting into when I started at ATPCo. Doug McDonald, the plant manager and one of Allen's close friends and business associates from the "old days," still had not changed his mode of operation from the original approach of twenty-five years before. He believed the "run it hard – fix it fast" process was the only way. Despite my many recommendations, all of which were rejected, we still hadn't emerged from the dark ages of plant maintenance. We were not getting any better; in fact, we were getting worse. The maintenance metrics used by the five plants clearly showed that we held a firm grip on last place. The pressure Allen was placing on Doug obviously flowed down to me to "fix the breakdowns faster." I just wished that there was a way I could convince Doug to have the plant operators "break the equipment slower."

That brings you up to today. My frustration with Doug and his poor management methods had become more and more apparent to me over the last few months. Not that I am a reliability expert. Yes, I had tried some preventive maintenance initiatives in my old plant. And, yes, with the help of my maintenance team, these initiatives had been successful. But in no way was I an expert. The point is that compared to Doug I was a PhD; hence, my increasing level of frustration. I was not even allowed to try the simplest activity such as checking oil levels or having the engineers identify the root causes of our continuous and repetitive failures. All I was ever told was, "get the equipment running as soon as possible" and my other favorite, "why aren't you done yet?" There was nothing that I or my maintenance team could do to satisfy my boss.

Just recently when the same pump failed for the third time, I decided to take matters into my own hands, whether Doug liked it or not. I knew that our #1 tractium line was being shut down for a process change. I seized the opportunity to conduct preventive maintenance on some of the problem equipment during the shutdown. I also didn't ask permission. My staff and our engineers planned the work in meticulous detail so that it would fit within the established outage duration set by Production. All of the work was scheduled for the evening shift, with the line set to be restarted in the morning. We scheduled ten mechanics to work overtime to perform the work. One of my foremen, who was as frustrated as I was, even agreed to stay over on his own time to supervise the work. With all of our preparation completed, I went home fully expecting to arrive the next morning and see that our initiative had succeeded. How could Doug deny the idea with the actual proof staring him in the face?

When I arrived at the plant and pulled into the parking lot I immediately knew something was wrong. The area where the maintenance mechanics parked had all of the regular cars parked in all of the regular spots including those that belonged to the mechanics and the supervisor who had stayed to work the preventive maintenance on the night shift. At the minimum, the mechanics' cars should not have been there; thcy should have been home sleeping. I thought for a moment that Nick, my foreman, had stayed to bring me up to date on the work accomplished, but I was wrong.

I didn't get very far past the main door when Nick walked past me. He didn't say hello and I could easily see from the look on his face that he was very upset.

"Wait a minute Nick," I said. "What's wrong?"

"Todd, we had just started work last night when Doug showed up on the line. He wasn't just angry, he was furious. He sent me and the crew home before we even got started working—something about unauthorized work without his permission. I was going to call you to warn you, but Doug said that if I did and he found out I would be fired. So I went home and guess what I got when I arrived at work this morning? A one-week suspension. I'll see you in a week if I can't find another job before then. I can't work for a person like Doug; I just hope I can find something better in such a short time. If not I'll be back but not for long"

My encounter with Nick was not a very good way to start the day, but things were about to get worse.

When I got to my office there was a very large note taped to my computer monitor. It obviously was from Doug, probably written as he was destroying the preventive maintenance initiative from the previous evening. It said;
See me immediately!
The message didn't leave me very much choice so I put down my briefcase and with some trepidation went to see Doug.

My arrival was expected and his administrative assistant immediately escorted me into his office. I knew he was angry, but decided not to say or do anything and see how the whole thing played out.

"Todd close the door and sit down," Doug said.

"What can I do for you, Doug?"

"I am sure you already know that I found out about your little experiment for Line #1 last evening. In fact I personally came back to the plant to put a stop to it and sent the crew home. I've dealt with Nick separately. Now I am going to deal with you."

"I have told you more than once that you need to clear all changes to the normal operating procedures with me before you take any action. Todd, you don't seem to ever listen. You did what I had expressly forbade you to do by setting up overtime and planning some half-baked preventive maintenance work on equipment that was running just fine. You seem to have conveniently forgotten that I am the manager of this plant, not you, and nothing gets initiated, especially some stupid pet program of yours without my prior approval. Is there something about this you fail to understand?"

At this point, I was so angry at this stupid petty bureaucrat with his narrow-minded approach that I thought best just too simply sit and say nothing because

if I had told him what I thought I would have been fired
on the spot.

"You and I have had a great number of disagree-
ments about how plant maintenance work should be
performed, but this is going to be the last time you do
something as blatant as this. You don't seem to remember that most of my career was spent as a maintenance
manager working for Allen. I know the equipment and
the job far better than you do." At this point Doug's face
was so red with anger that I thought he was prepared to
reach across his desk and choke me if he could have gotten away with it. I felt that I needed to say something in
my defense so I said, "Doug, just give me a chance to
explain." I didn't get any farther.

"Shut up and listen to what I am going to tell you
if you still want to be employed by ATPCo at the end of
this discussion," Doug said with a certain level of satisfaction evident in his voice as well as in his body language.

"Todd, I have had it with you and your ideas about
changing maintenance practices in my plant. If I had my
way, Security would be waiting at my door to escort you
out of the plant for good. However, Allen doesn't agree
with me and wants to give you one last chance. As of
right now you have two choices. First, the one I prefer is
for you to resign. The second is to relocate to the
Eastern Plant as maintenance manager. They have an
opening as a result of the resignation of the current manager. Maybe Mike Kane, the Eastern Plant manager, can
teach you how to properly run a maintenance department. The choice is yours. You need to give me your
answer tomorrow morning. Don't bother to come in, just
call. I really don't care to see you again. As for today, you

are suspended without pay. Now get out of my office, out of my plant, and out of my sight."

There was no doubt in my mind that our conversation, my work day, and possibly even my career at ATPCo were over. I wasn't simply angry; I was positively furious. How somebody like Doug could sit there while his plant and even the entire company were headed for oblivion was beyond my comprehension. On top of that, and at a more personal level, I was angry about how he had treated me, Nick, and others who were just trying to do a good job and improve the plant's reliability. How people like Doug ever got and stayed in positions of power was something that at that very moment I was finding hard to understand.

So I had a decision to make and the rest of the day to do it. It was only 8:30 in the morning but in the last few hours my world had changed. I knew that I needed to get out of the plant and calm down. I knew that I was going to go home but I also knew that I needed to have a clearer head before I did. An hour in the office cleaning up my personal effects would be just the ticket. So I went back to my office to gather my things, my laptop, and coat and to head home.

Doug's confrontation with me and his actions following my exit from his office had been well planned. I arrived at my office to find Security waiting. I knew both of the guys, but they reluctantly told me that, per Doug's explicit direction, I had to leave the plant immediately. I could come back for my personal things under escort tomorrow. The maintenance crew already knew what had happened to Nick so they didn't appear surprised at the events transpiring at my office.

This was the last straw. There was no need to treat

me like a common criminal, but Doug was making his point, not just for my sake, but to anyone who had any thought about taking any future action without his express approval.

So I left. Along the way, many of the maintenance crew stopped me and wished me luck. Many told me that if I found another job and needed mechanics to give them a call and they would be more than happy to leave ATPCo and join me. They thought that I was being fired. Through all of my mixed emotions at the time, I didn't say anything to change their beliefs.

Once in the car I calmed down a little bit and tried to organize my thoughts. I needed to go home and discuss my options with my wife. Together we needed to determine the answer I was going to give Doug in the morning. It was a long ride home because I was lost in thought considering and reconsidering the options. My wife Susan was surprised to see me and sat calmly as I explained what had happened. Of course that didn't happen for several hours until she had calmed herself down following my description of what Doug did to Nick and his treatment of me earlier.

In the end, the choice wasn't that difficult. I either resigned or relocated to the Eastern Plant. I could try to find another job, but we faced a tight job market in our area. We needed the income, so the move really was our only option. The selling point was that Susan's family lived within a one-day drive of the plant. By moving, she would be able to see more of them than she had in the last few years. For me, the selling point was that I would still have the same job and I would be as far away from Doug as I could possibly get. I didn't know at the time that I was moving from bad to worse; out of the frying pan into the fire. That realization didn't come until we had moved and I had started my new job.

Once the decision was made, we spent the rest of the day at a movie and an early dinner. By the time we arrived home, I was far less depressed and even looking forward to the new challenge. Before bed I decided to send Doug an e-mail telling him of my decision. I knew he wanted me to resign. I also knew he always checked e-mails before bed. I knew reading the e-mail that I was going to relocate would anger him and, hopefully, ruin the rest of his night. After sending the message to Doug I reviewed some of the other e-mails I had received during the day. Many were from co-workers wishing me luck. Some even went so far as to express their opinions about ATPCo and Doug. I erased them but felt glad that I was supported by the people I had worked with for the last five years. Just before getting up to shower, I noticed one e-mail that I had missed. It was from someone named TAN. The title read, "Todd, please read me." I thought that it might be spam but spam usually doesn't have your name in the title, so I opened it. The message read:

```
From: TAN
To: Todd Bradley

What happened to you today was
not the end, it was the begin-
ning. Reliability is the key to
your salvation.
```

This e-mail confused me. It had my name in the address and somehow the writer knew what had happened to me. A very strange situation, but I was tired and

could figure it out tomorrow, so Susan, Paws, and I went
to bed.

Out of the Frying Pan Into the Fire

The next few days flew by. I had forgotten since our last move over five years ago how difficult and stressful any move can be, let alone one completely across the country. After Susan and I had made arrangements to sell our house and hire a mover, we began packing. I don't save things. Susan, on the other hand, had managed to acquire a great deal since we moved in five years before. I managed to convince her to throw a lot of it away. As a result, we were easily able to fill a 20-cubic yard dumpster with what she kept telling me were her prized possessions. I even got her to throw away things in our attic that were still in the original boxes from our last move. A lot of these things we had completely forgotten even existed.

With all of the work in our now former home completed we flew east on a house hunting trip. We were fortunate not only to find a nice house in our price range, but one that was available for occupancy within one month. By the time we flew home again, we were satisfied that things had been prepared for our move on both ends. I had to report to the Eastern Plant the next week, so I left Susan to handle the move, expecting that she would join me within a week or two.

On Sunday I flew east. Monday morning found me at the reception desk of the Eastern Plant's main building. I was ready to get back to work, happy to start my new job, and equally happy to be 2500 miles away from Doug McDonald.

I introduced myself to the receptionist who had a look on her face that said she would rather be any place other than where she was at that moment. Have you ever run into someone who had that look about them? She proceeded to look my name up on the list she had on her PC and said, "So, you're the new maintenance manager. I wish you more luck than your predecessor had." I thought that her comment was rather presumptuous, but chalked it up to the fact that maybe she was just having a bad day.

"Mike is waiting for you but you need to clear

security, HR, and medical before I can take you over," she said. I was prepared for this process because it is the way everyone is processed whether they are a new employee or someone like me transferring from another site. It isn't that ATPCo is a security installation, but we need to make sure that those who we let into the plant are our employees. If not just for safety reasons, we also need to consider that some of our processes are secret.

After going through the standard processing and clearing several departments, I was ready. The receptionist escorted me as we made our way to Mike Kane's office. I thought that working for Mike had to be better than for Doug. After all, he had made time for me on his schedule and had informed my sour-faced receptionist that she was to bring me over as soon as I was processed. I figured that if he was that interested in me he couldn't be half bad.

As we approached the corner office, which I assumed to be Mike's, I started to hear a voice getting louder and louder as we got closer. By the time we reached the office waiting area, it wasn't just a loud voice. It was a voice that was screaming at someone. I couldn't make out many of the words, but some of them included stupid, incompetent, moron, and others of a more explicit nature that I won't repeat. This screaming was coming from inside Mike's office and my initial reaction was that whoever was on the receiving end must have done something very bad.

As I took my seat, being close to the door, I was able to hear more of the conversation.

"Why can't you keep my lines running? It's just a simple matter of producing tractium to meet the demands of our customers. But no, you can't seem to do even that. This job isn't rocket science. It just seems that you and your production team think it is, which makes all of you just plain stupid. I went home last evening and things were just fine. This morning, Line #1 is down and you don't even know why. What the hell is the matter with you? Remember, if you can't get it right, it's the highway for you and the rest of your incompetent cronies!"

"But Mike," was the feeble reply.

"Pat, you dumb #*^#@!!! Just keep the lines running. I have told you time and again how to run the operation. Last week I even showed you how to do it. You must really be totally incompetent. Now get out and get the lines back in service. Report in at your regularly scheduled time. Remember, do it my way or it's the highway!"

With that the door flew open. An ashen-faced person who I assumed was Pat emerged. He was visibly shaken and looked like he wanted to get far away from Mike and as quickly as he could.

"Lois, are you still there?"

"Yes Mike."

"Do you have our new maintenance manager with you and, if you do, bring him on in." She did as Mike asked and left almost as quickly as Pat.

And so I took my first step into Mike Kane's office. The man I saw there was relatively short, about 5'6", but very muscular. He had hard set eyes that looked like they could bore right through you. He was bald and looked like he was in his mid fifties, about the same age as Doug. That made sense because, just like Doug, Mike had been with Allen from the start of ATPCo 25 years earlier. He got up to welcome me and his hand shake nearly broke my hand. I winced and thought I could detect a slight grin on his face. I guess he was letting me know who was in charge. A great way to start!

I sat down and Mike got right to the point. "Todd, I have heard a lot about you recently from your former boss. Some good, but the majority not good. This is your last stop at ATPCo. You will make it here or you will be gone in short order. You are not going to pull any of that fancy PM stuff here. Let's be clear about one very important thing. I run this plant. It's my way or the highway. Understand?"

I must admit, he was very direct. I chose to simply nod and keep my mouth shut. I didn't much like the thought of the highway. We just moved here and I was determined to make a success of myself and my department. From the discussion I had just overheard between Mike and Pat. it sounded like the Eastern Plant could use some help.

"Todd, I run things around here. I know what to do and how to do it, so listen and learn. I have been doing this work from before tractium was even a recognized product, so I have a lot to teach you about how to do this work correctly. If you play ball, you will do just fine and we will get along. If you don't...." His voice trailed off as the phone rang.

"What? Line #3 just shut down again? I'll be right there!" Mike screamed into the phone. At least my first day at work wasn't going to be boring with at least two, maybe three, of the four lines down and production at a virtual standstill. So I stood up, figuring that I could go over to my office and then to the line to see what I could do to help the situation.

"Todd, you are not going anywhere except with me

right now. Let's go over to the line and I will show that stupid group of operators how to get the line running," Mike said as he hurried out the door. Not wanting to be left behind I hurried after him. On the production floor, I was immediately right at home. Allen had built each of the plants identically so it didn't matter which plant you were in; everything was the same. Very quickly we arrived at Line #3. I had hoped the problem would be minor—a little blockage or some other problem that could be cleared by the operators. I wish that had been the case. The main drive belt had failed, destroying itself as well as some of the other equipment that was in proximity to the failure. Fortunately no one was hurt.

The maintenance mechanics had already arrived and were beginning to clear away the debris. To my surprise, Mike climbed up onto the equipment and not only started to yell at the mechanics about what they should be doing, but also started to do some of the work himself. The maintenance supervisor on the job, who in my opinion had the problem under control when we arrived, stepped back and let Mike run the show. The look of utter frustration coupled with resignation on his face told the story. This wasn't the first and probably wouldn't be the last time this sort of thing had happened.

I needed to get to know the maintenance supervisor and now was as good a time as any, so I walked over and introduced myself. "Hi, I'm Todd Bradley the new maintenance manager. It looks like our team has their hands full. Do you have any idea what caused the belt failure?"

"Owen McGee, and I don't have any idea what happened. And now that Mike has destroyed any evidence, we probably never will. We actually had thought about disassembly in an orderly manner to try and determine the cause since this is a repetitive failure. Unfortunately, that is not how we work around here. The motto here is: just fix it! It's Mike's way or the highway," he said. The last part was said in a hushed voice so that Mike couldn't hear. It really wasn't necessary because by this time Mike and the mechanics were climbing all over the equipment grabbing broken parts and pieces of the failed belt and throwing them to the production floor.

This was an entirely new experience for me. I'd never seen a plant manager like Mike. Going out to the line to see what was being done was one thing. But doing what Mike was doing was something completely outside of my work experience. He was climbing over the equipment like a madman, and shouting at everyone as if that would help get the line back into production.

Just when I thought I had seen it all, he climbed down and began to scream at the operators. Once again, he threatened everyone in ear-shot with the highway. It crossed my mind that I would be hearing a lot about the highway in my future—just as long as I wasn't the one taking it. Mike next approached Owen and began to holler that maintenance should have started work sooner. Owen tried to explain that he got the crew to the job immediately but the line had to be made safe before he could allow anyone to go to work. That didn't satisfy Mike, who continued on his tirade until it seemed like he just ran out of energy. He then turned to me and said, "Let's go Todd. I'll drop you at your office on our way back."

My office was in the exact location as it had been in the Western Plant. Not only was it the same size, it also had the same furnishings and the same PC. When I said Allen standardized, I wasn't kidding.

As we got to the door, Mike pushed it open and said, "Enough chit-chat, get to work. Oh, by the way, don't even think about going home until you and your maintenance crews get the lines back in service. I don't care how long you have to stay. One last thing before I forget. Report to me every hour on the hour with a detailed status report about the plant's maintenance activities."

"Mike, do you still want me to report after the lines are running?" I said just to get some clarity on his request.

"Todd, you don't understand. I want the report every hour, every day, until I say 'otherwise,' and I won't be saying 'otherwise.'"

I was amazed. This man was definitely not going to let me run anything. There wasn't much I could say in answer to his directive and, anyway, he had already left! Rather than go into the office, I went back to Line #3 to seek out Owen and find out when he thought the line would be back in production. I found him in conversation with the operators and the maintenance crew. After introductions, he pulled me aside.

"Todd, the damage isn't really as bad as it looks. All we need to do is replace the belts and I've already sent some of the crew to the storehouse to get what we need. Fortunately we had the belts in stock. I'm glad I expedited a few new sets after we had the same failure two weeks ago. We also need to clean up the mess Mike made, which will add a few more hours, but we should be done by 4 o'clock."

"Thanks Owen. I'm going to head back to the office. Stop in when you get a chance and let's talk. I'd like to get to know you and the lay of the land around here."

Back at the office I decided to call Mike and let him know when the line would be back in service. Then I planned to walk over to Line #1 and see what the problem was that had shut them down earlier. I also hoped that I would run into Pat; I wanted to talk with him.

I dialed Mike's number. It was easy to find. I didn't even have to look in the company phone directory. My predecessor had written it on the wall above his desk, I guess so that he wouldn't forget it.

Lois answered, "Mike's been expecting your call. I'll put you through."

"Todd, Mike here, what's the story on Line #3? And by the way your call is six minutes late. I'll give you the benefit of the doubt since it's your first day, but when I say each hour I don't mean each hour give or take six minutes. Now when will Line #3 be back in production?"

"I talked to Owen and Line# 3 will be back up by 4. As soon as we are off the phone I will check on Line #1 and call you right back."

"Unacceptable. What kind of manager do you pretend to be? First, 4 o'clock is not good enough. I want Line #3 up and running by 2 at the latest. As for Line #1, as manager you should know when that line will be back up before you call me. Understood?"

Initially I didn't say anything in response. How could I have acquired all of the information he wanted. He had just left me about 30 minutes ago. If I was to survive here, I was going to have to figure out how to do better. My first day—no correction, my first half day—was not off to a very good start.

Finally I said, "Sorry Mike. I'll get right over to Line

#1, find out what their status is and call you back." I don't know if he even heard my last comment because he had hung up and the line was dead. On my way over to Line #1, I thought about Doug. Compared to Mike, Doug was an angel. I also had an old saying running through my mind and couldn't seem to shake it. It was "out of the frying pan, into the fire." I couldn't be sure, but I certainly suspected that I had been in the frying pan and now I was in the fire.

On my arrival at Line #1, I ran into Pat. We shook hands and introduced ourselves. It seems that Pat was the current production manager. He had recently been promoted from superintendent of Line #1 when Mike fired the last production manager three months ago. He commented that with the way things were going he thought he would be gone shortly. Line #1 was almost back up and running. The problem had been a tractium blockage caused by a failed control valve. To make conversation, I mentioned that those things happen sometimes and was surprised by Pat's response, "Not every week it doesn't. I told Mike we needed to upgrade that valve. The one we have is obsolete and we can't even buy parts, but he told me to stop complaining and make the one we had work. The new valve was only $1000. This line stop and all of the others caused by this valve are worth a whole lot more than a new valve, but as Mike says...." I finished the statement for Pat, "It's my way or the highway."

I stayed around for about ten minutes watching the production and maintenance crew's work. When the line finally started, I went back to my office to report once again to Mike. Owen was waiting for me and sat patiently while I reported in and got my share of abuse.

At least the Line#1 was back in production with Line #3 to follow shortly.

When I had finished I got Owen and myself a cup of coffee and we sat down to get acquainted. Owen was the superintendent of the execution as well as the planning portions of the maintenance organization. This role made him Mike's whipping boy since the departure of the former maintenance manager. I got the distinct impression that he was somewhat relieved to see me because he now could transfer his "whipping boy" responsibilities to me.

"Todd, you seem like a nice guy who really knows the business. I've spoken with some of the people I know at the Western Plant and they have more than confirmed this to be true. You have absolutely no idea what you have gotten yourself into out here. Doug gave you a choice of leaving ATPCo or coming here. In my humble opinion, you made the wrong decision." Hearing this from one of my key supervisors made me feel wonderful and had me looking forward to all of the fun-filled days in my future.

"If that's the case, Owen, then why are you still here?" I asked.

"I have no choice. The benefits are good and so is the pay. I can't say the same thing about the working conditions, but I need the money and especially the benefits for personal reasons. So I take the abuse and stay on. That's not the case with a great many others. The production manager was fired, the last maintenance manager quit, and if you looked at the entire list of former line operators, mechanics, engineers, and even office workers you would be amazed. The older people stay because they have to; the younger people don't last.

The sad part is that it wasn't so bad before Mike. Our former manager was a good person, well liked by the organization, and he got the job done. Mike only got the job because he was Allen's friend and had worked with him from the beginning."

"OK, so the working conditions are bad, but what is the condition of the equipment? I haven't even been here one day and already two lines have shut down."

"Todd, we go day-to-day in the exact mode of operation that you saw this morning. The best days are when Mike doesn't show up to help us do our jobs," he said. "Not only that, but with all of the downtime, production levels have fallen short of the contracted demand. Because of this, we recently lost one of our major contracts. If you think Mike was angry this morning you should have seen him then."

"Wow, the situation sounds really bad. Is anything being done to correct some of these problems? Even the things I saw today could be corrected with a little reliability-focused effort." Owen didn't have to answer, but he did.

"No, nothing is done to remedy the problems. It's 'run it hard – fix it fast.' That's how we work, or it's the highway. We don't do any planning; in fact my planners are actually material expediters for the emergencies. We don't even pretend to follow a work schedule. Basically everyone just sits around waiting for the alarm."

"What alarm is that," I asked.

"You'll see or, should I say, hear. Mike had alarms installed on the production floor so that if a line goes down, everyone knows it and is required to respond. You didn't hear it this morning because it doesn't sound in the office. We thought about installing an alarm in Mike's office, but he would rather shoot the messenger."

Our discussion lasted for over an hour, at which time I needed to call Mike again and assure him that everything was still running. This time my call was exactly on the hour. I gave my report and Mike never said a word. He just listened and, when he assumed I was through, he hung up. I now had a whole hour before my next report to walk around, observe the operation, and meet the people. I also wanted to find Pat. I wanted to get his opinion of the production side of the operation as well as the reliability of the equipment. I knew his view would be more focused on production, but I also knew that if the equipment failed to operate, then ATPCo didn't produce and couldn't stay in business.

As I walked through the plant I was able to take note of many things. First and foremost, the people were not happy. It was evident in the demeanor and the disinterested way in which they carried out their work. They weren't even interested when I introduced myself as the new maintenance manager. I would have expected some comments about how maintenance could improve. Production people always have ideas along these lines, but the people I talked with could care less. I also noticed that the plant wasn't clean. There was a great deal of debris, trash, and the normal things that are part of a production process that when used get properly discarded —only they weren't, they were just lying there on the production floor. It even looked like some maintenance jobs had been started and then abandoned, left in an unfinished state for some future return of the work crew. Knowing what I had learned so far I suspected that they had been pulled off to some emergency. The plant was in a sorry state.

All of a sudden the loudest alarm I had ever heard began sounding. I counted the tones; there were four tones repeated over and over. One of the mechanics I had just met ran past. I knew something was wrong, but not what. He turned and yelled to me trying to be heard above the alarm, "Line #4 is down, come on!" So I and virtually everyone around me ran to the shutdown line. This certainly wasn't standard process from any experience I had ever had; this was something entirely new. At least I now knew what Owen meant by the alarm.

I turned the corner at Line #4 and ran into Pat. "What's happening?"

Pat just pointed. The same belts that failed on Line #3 were lying shredded in the aisle next to Line #4. Mike had reached the line before me and was already directing the work and simultaneously screaming at everyone in sight. Once again the maintenance crews stated working on replacing the belts. When everything had calmed down, meaning Mike had left the job, Pat and I walked back to his office and he closed the door. I don't think I have ever seen a grown man so close to tears. I just sat there not knowing what to say to help the situation.

"Todd, did you offend some tractium god who decided to punish you and send you to Hell? Because that's where you are! This place is a nightmare. Everyday we patch the equipment and things just get worse. I don't know what to do. I can't seem to run the lines correctly, and in general can't do anything else right either – at least according to Mike. I really wish I could go back to my former job on the line, but Mike won't allow it. I know it's just your first day, but have you any ideas of what we can do?"

"I wish I did, Pat. I do have to admit that I thought

the Western Plant was bad, but it was a country club compared to this place. Give me a chance to get more familiar with the plant and the work, and maybe we can figure something out to help our situation." I wanted to stay longer but I had to report to Mike.

The balance of the day was uneventful, unless you consider getting yelled at for something I didn't even know about as significant.

Oh yes, one more thing. Remember the strange e-mail I got the day Doug kicked me out. Well I got another one as I was getting ready to leave for the day. This one said the same thing;

 From: TAN
To: Todd. Bradley

Reliability is the key to your salvation.

There was that message again. This was very disturbing because TAN, whoever he was, knew my name and, even stranger, knew I had relocated to the Eastern Plant. I deleted the message and went back to my hotel to call Susan and see how she was doing. I didn't plan to tell her yet about all of the fun I was having at work. Her efforts to coordinate the move were stressful enough. It was now 6:00 PM, all of the lines were finally back in service, and I felt as if I had been at work forever. On my way out, I could see that the light in Mike's office was still on.

LIFE GETS MORE INTERESTING

Several weeks later after Susan had sold the house and supervised the packing and the move, she joined me at my hotel. It was terrific to see her. The weeks I had spent without her, her counsel, and her support had been difficult. The phone discussions were always short and I avoided telling her much of what was happening at work. I didn't want to upset her. However, once she joined me all of the issues and problems that I had been bottling up spilled out. We agreed that for now we would try our best to stick it out, but we were equally aware that I couldn't keep working in this manner and retain my health and my sanity. Shortly thereafter, we moved into our new home and tried to re-establish our lives.

My days turned into weeks and weeks into months. Every day was the same. After a while, it all ran together into an insane blur of failed equipment, failure to meet production quotas, and the chaos of working for Mike Kane. Before I knew it six months had passed.

Then one day everything changed. I received a call from Lois to report immediately to Mike's office. That in itself was strange. All of my contacts with Mike had been during my hourly status reports over the phone, our encounters during line shutdowns, and other related emergencies that brought Mike to the production floor. Seldom was I ever summoned to his office.

On my way to Mike's office I ran into Pat. "Do you know what's going on? I hardly ever get called to Mike's office; certainly not for something good anyway. The immediate part makes it even stranger still. At least I'm not the only one in trouble since we're both on the same mission," I added with very little humor in my voice.

"I have no idea what this is all about." Pat replied. "Maybe we are both getting fired or worse getting to stay on," Pat said with a sly grin.

The only thing I could think of worse than having to go to Mike's office was having to go there on a regular basis; I hoped this wasn't going to be my new routine. When we arrived, Lois sent us both right in. Mike was sitting at his desk with teleconference equipment spread out on his desk.

"Sit down. Allen will be on the line in a minute. He

called earlier and said he wanted to speak with all of us about something of great importance to ATPCo. He could have told me. I don't have any idea why he felt he needed you two incompetents as well."

Just then there was a beep tone and Allen was on the line. "Gentlemen," he said. "We have a problem. A new form of tractium has been developed which can be used not only for products in the home but also for industry. I am not sure how it was named, but everyone is calling it Epsilon. It isn't entirely different from what we currently manufacture; it just has some unique additives. As a result, it will require modifications to the line that is going to produce it. That's the good news – just a modification to the equipment and we are in production.

The bad news is that the emerging market for this product is dead center in the area where the Eastern Plant manufactures and markets our products, and you can't even manufacture tractium to meet your current quotas and contract requirements. The further bad news is that the cost to manufacture Epsilon is so tight that making it anywhere else in our plant network and shipping it to you is not economical. Actually it is impossible. So you see we have serious issues here."

Pat and I looked at each other and then at Mike. I had never seen him look like this before, even when he was out on the line screaming at someone when the line went down. He was visibly shaking and his hands were trembling. His reaction wasn't that hard to understand. He was operating a plant in the heart of a new product market. Yet he couldn't keep the plant running to manufacture the existing products, let alone a new one. Actually for Mike it was even worse. Allen was not just his boss; Allen was his friend. He was the person who

Mike had supported as they struggled to build the company. Now Mike was about to let Allen down in a really big way. So big that when I considered the issues I realized our failure could put the company out of business. But Allen wasn't finished. "We have received a request from a new customer. Their name is not nearly as important as what they have requested. They want a group of suppliers for Epsilon that they can count on to reliably deliver the product. For ATPCo, this would be a major contract that would have the potential of doubling our revenue. The hitch is that they have assembled a team to review the companies and specific plants that could manufacture Epsilon for them. They want to be sure that whoever they select can meet their demand, not just some of the time, but all of the time. In other words, they want a partner who is reliable. Their inspection team will be visiting the Eastern Plant in 90 days.

Mike, we need this contract. It is the key to our long-term viability. I know that you are having problems, but I feel confident that you can work your way through them and win this contract. I'll give you a week to devise a detailed plan and call you back so we can review it. This is a big deal, Mike. Don't let me down." With that he hung up.

Mike never did get to tell us how he was going to solve the plant's problems and win the contract for Allen and ATPCo because the Line Down alarm went off at that very moment. Since I had started at the Eastern Plant, the failure of our equipment had become so routine that Mike had the alarm installed in his office; before he had simply been called on the phone. Funny thing, I didn't even jump anymore when the alarm went off because it was such a common occurrence. This time it was Line #3 again. Before I could even get up, Mike was out the door and on his way.

I looked over at Pat and could almost read his mind. He confirmed this fact when he said what I had also been thinking, "We don't have a prayer." I had to admit that I certainly agreed.

We arrived at Line #3 only to see the same events transpiring as had taken place so many times in the past. I could no longer even count the number of times. The operators and the mechanics were working on the line repair while Mike alternated between screaming at anyone near enough for him to grab and helping, or should I say disrupting, the repair process.

Of course, just like every other time, we got the line running again. By the time we were finished, it was late so I made my final report to Mike and headed out the gate. During my final status report of the day, Mike indicated that he would be ready in the morning with a detailed plan, one that would tell Pat and me how we were going to make the plant more reliable. I could hardly wait for the details. Of course, Mike never asked for any input. If he had, I could have given him a few ideas.

I arrived home and told Susan what had happened related to the new product and the call from Allen. She doesn't know much about the business, but is a very perceptive person. It was her conclusion that we should start looking for a new job. With the current plant situation and our need to produce Epsilon reliably for the new client, we were essentially dead; we just hadn't recognized the fact yet. I have to admit that I agreed with her just as I had agreed with Pat earlier.

About 11 o'clock, we had been asleep for about an

hour, when the phone rang. A ringing phone in the middle of the night was not an unusual part of my routine. Plant emergencies during the night shift were just as much an issue as emergencies during the day. Struggling to wake up, I picked up the phone expecting it to be the night foreman with some critical problem that couldn't wait until morning. I was in no mood for the call but it was part of my fun-filled job.

"Todd, it's Pat. I'm sorry to bother you, but something has happened."

"Can't it wait until morning or is this one of Mike's 'it has to be done right now mandates?'" Pat could tell from the tone of my voice that I wasn't happy getting called in the middle of the night about some plant problem that Mike felt needed immediate attention.

"Todd, it's not about the plant. It's about Mike. He had a massive heart attack and died a few hours ago. Allen just called me to tell me the news. Allen wants us to teleconference with him first thing in the morning."

I was dumbstruck and just stood there until Susan asked what was wrong. "Mike's dead," was all that I could say. Then I realized Pat was still on the phone. "Pat, I'll meet you at the plant at seven. Where should we meet?" I asked.

"We might as well meet at Mike's office," Pat said. "He has the teleconference equipment in his closet."

Needless to say, I couldn't immediately get back to sleep. When I finally did, all that I was able to do was to toss and turn. There was just too much going on in my mind: Mike's death, the plant problems, and even more importantly what were we going to do to resolve them. Susan was as upset as I was about what had happened. Granted she didn't like Mike, but no one wanted something like this to happen, even to someone who was as unlikable as Mike Kane. Because neither of us was really sleepy, we got up, made some coffee, and spent the rest of the night discussing what had happened and my future in a world without Mike Kane.

I got to the plant early the next day, an hour earlier than my usual arrival time. I must have looked a sight, having gone with very little sleep, but Pat and I had a lot of preparation to do before our 10 o'clock teleconference with Allen. Fortunately we were on the east coast and Allen on the west. So even if he got to work early, we still had a few hours to consider what we were going to describe to him as our path to move forward. I had some time before Pat was expected to arrive so I thought I would clean up some e-mails from the previous day. I started up my PC and there it was again—this must have been the fifth or sixth time I got the same message.

From: TAN
To: Todd Bradley

Reliability is the key to your salvation.

This time, unlike all of the others in the past, I didn't just delete the message. I did something very very different. I answered it.

From: Todd Bradley
To: TAN

OK. So if reliability is the key to my salvation, where do I start? We certainly could use

help, even if it is from some
unidentified person via e-mail.

I hit the send button expecting that whoever was
sending the e-mails, once they were asked for some
information, would go away. Not so. What I received was
an immediate response.

 From: TAN
To: Todd Bradley

You start with a vision of your
future. Knowing how bad things
are now, you need to create a
simple statement for everyone,
not just for you and Pat, that
paints a crystal clear picture
of what a really good and highly
reliable plant can look like.
Oh, by the way, when you figure
out what your vision is send it
to me. I probably can help you
fine tune it.

Having an e-mail dialog with someone I did not
know was strange. Even stranger was that this person
was giving me advice that seemed to be very sound. I
didn't get much time to consider it because I needed to
get over and see Pat. We needed to deal with Mike's
death as well as the fact that in 90 days a major potential
customer was going to visit us. The customer expected
to see a reliable plant in operation if we ever hoped to
get their business.

Arriving at Mike's office gave me an incredibly
bizarre feeling. I expected to see Mike sitting at his desk,

ready to tell me one more time how incompetent I was and how he could run the maintenance organization far better. However, that wasn't the case. Mike was gone. In his place was Pat looking like the end of the world was fast approaching; maybe it was. Allen was going to call. He would expect us to tell him our initial plan related to improving plant reliability and converting the equipment to Epsilon manufacturing.

I had hardly greeted Pat and sat down when the phone rang. Pat answered. Allen was early; it must have been about 5 AM on the west coast.

"Yes, Allen. Todd and I are both here. We were waiting for your call. I'll put it on speaker."

"Pat, Todd," Allen said. "This is a sad day for ATPCo and even more so for me on a very personal level. I worked with Mike since we started this company. We went through everything together—the good as well as the bad. I for one am going to miss him greatly. Pat, please stay in contact with Mike's family. Let them know that if they need anything, anything at all, I'll see that they get it. Also, I will be flying in for the funeral as will all of the other plant managers, as well as some of Mike's old friends from the other sites. Now on to business," Allen said.

"Pat, I don't have someone available to take over the plant manger's job who knows as much about the operation as you do. With the customer's 90-day review and the associated contract on the line, I wish I did, but I don't. Pat I need you to temporarily assume the duties of plant manager and get the place in shape. Todd, I expect that you will give Pat your full support in this effort. We absolutely must have the plant running reliably so that the customer can see us at our best. We need that Epsilon contract and we need it bad. Can I count on you to get the job done?"

Pat looked like he was about to join Mike. His face was as white as a ghost and he looked scared. Nevertheless, he managed to say, "Allen, you can count on me and the team here at the Eastern Plant."

After reminding us that he wanted a plan in a week, Allen hung up the phone. Pat said, "What are we going to do? A little less than a year ago, I was just a line superintendent. Now through no doing of my own, I find myself as acting plant manager. Not only that, but I have to take the most unreliable plant on the face of the earth, change everything around, and show a potential customer that we can deliver Epsilon on time every time. And to make matters worse, if that is even possible, I have to do it in 90 days. Like I said, what are we going to do?"

Did you ever have one of those experiences where the proverbial light bulb went on in your head? Well that was what happened to me at that very moment. As if by magic, I connected what TAN had said in his e-mail with our immediate problem. So I sat back and said, "Pat we need to start with a vision of the Eastern Plant's future. We need to determine what we want this place to look like when our prospective customer shows up. Not only that, but what do we want the plant to look like after we get the contract, and further out into the future?"

All of a sudden Pat's face brightened up. "Why didn't I think of that," he said. "Todd, that's a great place to start. What do you think our vision should say?

Notice I didn't tell him about the e-mail. He probably wouldn't have believed it anyway. I had a good picture in my own mind, but found it hard to articulate.

Furthermore, I didn't want it to be just my vision. I wanted it to be something we created together and could both believe we could accomplish. So we talked about what we believed a highly reliable plant would look like, not just for our customers, but for the people who had to come to work each day and relied on ATPCo and the Eastern Plant for their livelihood. After a while we decided that our vision would be:

> *To operate our facility in a way that*
> *enables us to always meet the*
> *production demands of our customers.*

We believed that, if we could operate in this manner, we could be successful. The plant would be running reliably; it would be able to supply tractium, Epsilon, or any of the other tractium products to our customers. I wrote the vision down and headed back to my office. I left Pat alone to prepare for officially notifying everyone what had happened to Mike and for communicating that he would be taking over Mike's duties. The news about Mike had already been handled unofficially by the gossips and the rumor mill. As for Mike's successor, no one really cared, expecting that things would just go on as they had under Mike.

When I got to my office, I closed the door and did what many of you may consider a very strange thing. I sent the vision we had written to TAN. After all, TAN had been the one to suggest creating a vision in the first place. I didn't expect a response, but within an hour I got one.

From: TAN
To: Todd Bradley

Your vision is weak. It doesn't
paint a clear picture of the
future. You need to do better
than what you sent to me. I'll
bet you didn't even spend an
hour on it and, worse, probably
never asked anyone for input.
Get back to me when you have
something worthwhile to review.

I stared at the e-mail for a few minutes without any reaction. Who was this person, how did they know who I was, and why were they giving me advice? Of course, there was no answer to these questions. After some further consideration of what our vision should say, I went to check on the lines.

As I walked around I kept thinking more and more about our plant and what our vision of the future should be. Everyone was talking about Mike's death and I was asked many questions which I answered to the best of my ability. Many of these were about Mike, but some were about Epsilon and our possible new customer. The workforce even knew about the 90-day review.

Walking through the plant and talking with the workers got me thinking. I wondered what they would say the vision of the future should be if I asked them. So, guess what. I asked! Not just one person, but everyone I saw who was willing to talk to me. My questioning created a lot of discussion and quite a bit of surprise from many. One mechanic summed it up for me when he thanked me for asking and said, 'I've worked here for over fifteen years and this is the first time anyone ever asked me what I thought."

This process took a long time, but when I was finished I had talked with more than 50 people. I had obtained a lot of ideas, all of which were spinning around in my head. By this time it was 6 o'clock; I packed up and headed home.

That night I couldn't sleep again. I could think only about all of those people in the plant and their ideas of what our future should look like. The more I thought about it, the more a very strong feeling grew inside me. Pat and I had to deliver not simply a vision, but a reliability reality for everyone. And we had to do it in 89 days!

The next morning I went to see Pat again. It was a sad day because Mike's funeral was scheduled for that afternoon. We had only a brief opportunity to talk about the vision because Allen and the other managers were due at the airport at 11 o'clock; Pat and I were going to pick them up. However in our brief discussion, I told him what I had done the prior day. Pat said that he thought I was headed in the right direction and wanted to hear more, but we were out of time.

I realized that if you want a vision people can adopt, in this case as one that creates a reliability-based future, it probably is a good idea to ask them what they think. In doing so, I had inadvertently taken a step towards getting universal buy in. People liked the idea that I had asked them; they also liked the idea that someone thought their thoughts had value. These ideas were a far change from the world according to Mike.

The rest of the day was a blur that culminated with a late afternoon funeral. There were several brief speeches from Allen and the other managers who had worked with Mike. As I listened to all of the praise heaped upon Mike, and based on what I knew of the man from the last six months, I wondered if we were really burying Mike Kane. Many of the people from the plant were also in attendance, but I wasn't sure if they were there out of respect or just to make sure Mike was really going.

Susan was there as well. She had never met Mike, but disliked him intensely for all of the things he had done to me over the last six months. She cried during the service in spite of her feelings about Mike. I have always found Susan to have a warm and giving heart, more so than anyone I've ever known. Mike's funeral proved that for me ten times over.

As we were leaving the cemetery, we literally bumped into Doug. I had been avoiding any contact with him for obvious reasons, but in this case there was no way of avoiding saying something. My biggest fear was what Susan was going to say or, even worse, do.

"Hello Doug, how are you?" I said.

"Todd, I'm surprised to see you survived six months," was all he said. Not even "I'm glad to see you" or simply "How are you doing?" This guy hadn't changed a bit. He was still the same miserable person as when I had worked for him.

Susan's comeback surprised me and certainly was totally unexpected. I had just expected her to ignore the man. However, she said, "Now that Mike is gone and we are no longer subject to your poor management style, just wait and see what Todd is going to accomplish." With that she turned and walked away, leaving me to have to hurry to catch up. Life certainly was getting more interesting.

The Vision and More Take Shape

The first thing that I did the next morning was to make sure that the day's emergencies were handled. I then headed to Pat's office. I had spent the prior evening organizing my notes regarding my discussions with the workforce about our plant's vision of the future. I added my thoughts and as a result had a substantial list of ideas that could be included in the vision we needed to develop. It was interesting to me how many good ideas were suggested by the workforce. It also amazed me how virtually untapped this resource was. I made up my mind not to overlook their value in the future.

Near Line #2 I ran into Gene Smith, the union president. Our plant had a union, but fortunately not many union issues other than those that had been caused by Mike. As a result of the production-related confrontations that Mike had instigated, Pat had experienced a difficult time working with Gene. On the other hand, my interaction with Gene had been mostly cordial, just working out issues such as job assignments and overtime. Under different circumstances, Gene and I could have been friends simply because we really loved the company and the people. However, we needed to maintain the union–management relationship, so a friendship would have to wait for some other time.

"Todd," Gene said. "I have heard that the day before the funeral you were going throughout the plant asking everyone what they thought the vision of our future should look like. I'll have to admit that this was the first time in my recollection that anyone ever asked the workforce, and even some of the supervisors what they thought about anything. You have a lot of people talking. They know about the reliability problems we have here. After all, they live with them every day.

"They also know about Epsilon and the site visit in less than three months. Many are skeptical and, as you can guess, the rumor mill is running wild. Many believe we are being sold and others that we are being shut down. I hope neither of these rumors comes true.

"Todd, I believe that you have the best interests of

the plant and the workers at heart. I want to believe that you and Pat are going to fix things. I just wanted to tell you that I hope you succeed. We are counting on you; don't let us down. Oh, one more thing. Make sure that in your vision you have something about the value each individual can bring to the organization." Without any further comment, Gene turned and walked away.

At that minute, the Line Down Alarm went off again. I had to delay visiting Pat, but I sincerely hoped to sit and talk with him before the day was out. My wish was granted; we got lucky. This time the problem with the line was minor and I found myself in Pat's office within the hour. We closed the door and spent the next several hours reviewing my notes and crafting what we considered was going to be the vision of the Eastern Plant. What we developed was:

> *We will operate our plant so that equipment never fails in an unplanned fashion. This high level of reliability will enable us to continually supply the demand of our customers as well as take on new ones. We will perform this work in a way that recognizes the important and unique value that each person brings to the effort.*

When we were done it was late in the afternoon. We both felt proud of our effort but recognized that the vision needed to be embraced by everyone if it were going to be successfully implemented. As strange as it may sound, I wanted to send it to TAN and get a reaction. TAN's advice about the vision had been sound. If the truth be told, we certainly needed all the help we could get with the next steps.

So I went back to the office and sent the e-mail. I certainly didn't expect an immediate reply. In fact, I wasn't sure that I would get any reply at all. I still had a lot of catching up to do with paperwork that had built up while we were attending Mike's funeral. I dove right into my backlog and was lost in the paper shuffle process when, taking a breather, I noticed that TAN had responded.

 From: TAN
To: Todd Bradley

Good job. Now what? A vision needs to be shared and believed in by everyone. That is why it is usually called a collective vision. Let me know what your next steps are going to be.

The question posed by TAN was the same one that Pat and I had wrestled with earlier in the day. In fact, we had decided on a course of action. We were going to print up copies of the vision, hold a plant meeting, and review the vision with the organization. We had even taken the step of scheduling the meeting for noon the next day. I explained all of this to TAN in my response. At this time, however, Pat and I had not done any planning beyond holding the meeting and making the announcement. I was more than aware of this and TAN quickly picked up on our lack of preparedness.

 From: TAN
To: Todd Bradley

Making an announcement of your

vision is an absolutely worthless exercise unless you show
the organization that the vision
of the future is going to become
a reality for them.

Did you ever wonder why dedicat-
ed people working in terrific
companies introduce change initiatives that fail to deliver
the lofty goals stated at the
outset? Some of these initiatives fail to deliver on all the
goals, and many fail completely.
The former is bad enough; the
latter is worse because total
failure leaves a skeptical
organization in its wake. In
turn, a skeptical organization
will resist another change initiative for a very long time.
Why? Because the failed initiative is one that the workers
supported passionately, hoping
that collectively they could
improve the functioning of the
business. Why risk such failure
a second time?

Todd, before we go any further,
I think you need to learn about
the Eight Elements of Change and
the Four Elements of Culture.

Change fails mainly for one reason. That reason is that those

who initiate the change initiatives work and think only at
what I will call the "hard
skill" level.
Hard skills are those tasks we
perform every day as part of our
jobs. Examples include reactive
and even proactive maintenance.
Trying to change or improve one
of these tasks is a superficial
approach to change and usually
leads to failure of the change
initiative. Think of hard skill
change as the top of a pyramid.
Below this level are two others
that support it. Failing to
address these levels will lead
to failure of the initiative
and, in turn, the skeptical
workforce I referred to previously. These two other levels,
which are the foundations for
hard skill change, are called
the soft skills and the organizational culture.

The soft skill level is composed
of intangible elements, which
are very different from the hard
skills that they support. There
are different names for the soft
skills, but they can all be summarized in a set called the
Eight Elements of Change. These
elements are very important
independently but are even more

important when they are all
linked together as a collective
whole. The eight elements are
leadership, work process, structure, group learning, technology, communication, interrelationships, and rewards. Let me
briefly describe each of these
so that you can get a feel for
what they deliver to the change
process.

Leadership is the most important
element. Without leadership at
all levels, the organization
will not be able to stay on
course. Leaders set the tone. If
that tone is set on a consistent
basis, the organization will
begin to believe that the work
processes can change and, even
more important, they can stay
changed.

However leadership is not something that can be demonstrated
just once, then ignored. Your
presentation of the vision
developed by you and Pat is just
the tip of the iceberg. You, the
plant manager, and all, yes all,
of the people the organization
looks to for guidance must
actively support and follow the
vision each and every day. As
soon as anyone with a leadership

role fails to adhere to the vision, the organization will start to lose faith. It then starts down the road to failure.

For example, consider the manager who preaches safety but then, in order to increase production, ignores an unsafe act. Failure to follow your own vision will instantly be recognized and your vision will lose credibility. Undermine your vision a number of times and those who believed will cease to believe. Therefore, leaders who "walk the talk" are a critical component of any successful change initiative.

The next element is **work process.** Think about how you do your work now or, even better, consider how it was done when Mike was alive. The process was totally reactive. With a reactive work process in place, how can you ever hope to implement a reliability-focused work process? The answer is that it cannot be done. For change to be successful — especially one that will move ATPCo from where you are now to one in which equipment never fails without advance notice and one in which all

repairs are conducted to eliminate future failures — you need
a sound reliability-focused work
process.

The third element is **structure.**
Once you have a reliability-
focused process, you need an
organizational structure to support it. Work process and structure go hand-in-hand. The manner
in which ATPCo is organized now
would never support your reliability vision. You don't have
enough people focused on reliability. The planning and execution organizations are not
aligned; they have no idea of
their roles and responsibilities
in the new process.

Roles and responsibilities are
an important part of structure.
You can assign the best people
to the correct blocks in the
organization chart. However, if
they are not clear on their
roles and responsibilities within the structure, then either
they will do redundant and often
conflicting tasks or the work
will not get done at all.

Group learning is another critical element. You and those you
work with need to learn from

your successes and failures. If
you don't, you will repeat your
mistakes. You may not even recognize why the work that you are
doing never seems to drive the
improvement that you seek. Many
people fail to grasp the real
depth of this element. You may
remember using the feedback loop
diagram in college. Applied to
group learning, the diagram
looks like the one that follows.

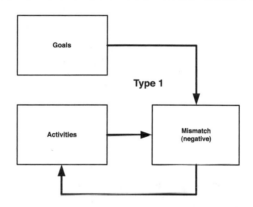

You set your goals and work to
achieve them by performing various activities. As these activities are completed, you review
the outcome of the activity vs.
the goal, identify the gaps, and
take corrective action by
adjusting your activities. If
you follow all these steps, then
the next time you perform the
revised activity it is closer in
line with your goal.

Single loop learning is fine by itself, but it may not be enough. You also need to examine your goals. What if they are wrong? Consider the world of Mike Kane. In this case, the single feedback loop is telling you that you need to get better at fixing the equipment faster. You already know the outcome of that approach; you are living with it right now. I suggest that you consider the following model instead. It requires that on a periodic basis you examine your goals as well, not just the activities. This model is called Type 2 learning.

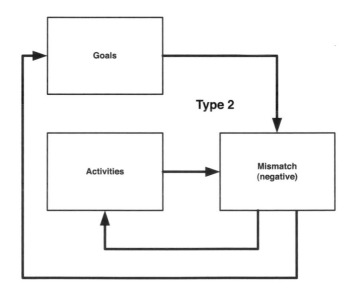

Todd, if you think about it, you are already using this model. You and others recognize that "run it hard / fix it fast" doesn't work if you are trying to promote a reliability-focused plant. Keep this model firmly in your mind and take the time periodically to run a reality check on your goals.

Technology is the next element. I'm not referring just to the sophisticated hardware that ATPCo uses to run the business, or to the people who populate that part of the organization. Instead, by technology I mean the software and some of the hardware used by the maintenance department to conduct their part of the business. With the sophisticated levels of work processed by a computerized maintenance management system and the other supporting applications you use, these tools become a critical part of the business. Therefore, technology is considered one of the eight elements of change.

The next element is **communication.** As you are already aware from your plans tomorrow to communicate the vision to the

organization, communication is a
critical element in the change
process. However, you need to
realize that communication must
be continuous. Furthermore, it
can't be one way; communication
needs to be bi-directional.

Without constant and continuous
communication to the workforce,
people will not know what is
happening as the change initiative is deployed. Because change
is dynamic, you need to have a
constant level of communication
so that workers are constantly
informed. Otherwise there will
be gaps in the flow of information, and people will create
information, whether true or
not, to fill the voids.

Additionally communication must
be two way. When you communicate, you expect others to listen. Similarly when your employees tell you things, you need to
listen to them. Not only do both
sides need to listen, but they
need to make sure that they
understand what was said. I
think you have taken a positive
step in that direction by asking
people about their idea for a
vision for the Eastern Plant.
When you communicate the vision

to them tomorrow, they will judge the content to see if you were actually listening to them. The seventh of the eight elements is **interrelationships.** This one is easy to understand if you consider Doug and Mike as two exceptionally "bad" examples. Their behavior certainly didn't help build good interrelationships. In fact, they created organizations with exactly the opposite behavior. Always remember that people come to work to earn a living. If the interrelationships they have at work are positive, then they will like their jobs, be more productive, and, yes, be more open to change. The road to success in the world of change is to treat people with dignity and respect.

Last but not least are **rewards.** When people hear the word rewards, the first thing that they usually think about is money. Well, money is a reward of sorts, but it usually doesn't have a long-lasting effect. The rewards I am describing are rewards associated with feeling good about the work you do and the value that you and your co-workers add to the business.

When (notice I didn't say if) you succeed in helping the plant become more reliable and you win the Epsilon contract, you will truly understand what I mean about rewards.

The eight elements of change are the first level of foundational support for hard skill change, but it is not the end of the story. There is that other level I mentioned called the organizational culture. Just as the soft skill level has eight elements, the cultural level has four, called the Four Elements of Culture. Like the eight elements of change, the four elements of culture are independently important, but even more important as a collective set. However, before I describe the individual elements, let me first define what I mean by the term organizational culture. Actually, this definition is not mine, but one developed by E. Schein in his book entitled Organizational Culture and Leadership:

"A pattern of <u>shared basic assumptions</u> that the *group learned as it solved its problems* of external adaptation and internal integration <u>that has</u>

worked well enough to be considered valid and, therefore, to be
taught to new members as the
correct way to perceive, think,
and feel in relation to those
problems."

Think hard about the parts that
I have underlined for you. Also
consider how a culture like the
one Mike had established could
take hold at the Eastern Plant.
It should be easy for you to
recognize that Mike promoted the
culture and dictated how people
thought, felt, and acted. Then
consider how difficult it will
be for you, Pat, and others to
change the culture, even when
people recognize it isn't the
most optimal way to act. I think
you will agree that your task is
going to be very difficult, but
of course not impossible.

Let's move on to the components
of culture.

The first of these is **organizational values**. Values are how we
act individually and organiza-
tionally in varying circumstances; usually without any
forethought. They are behaviors
that are ingrained in how we
work and in everything we do. At

work they can be initially set by the leaders. Over time, however, these values become validated as "how work is performed" and they are continually reinforced by both management and the workforce. In fact, they become so ingrained that these behaviors are taught to all new members as how to work if you want to succeed. Don't think for a minute that the "break it / fix it" culture left the plant with Mike. It is ingrained and it will be your job to instill a new culture in the plant.

Part of the new culture or the continuation of the old will be reinforced by the **role models**, the second of the four elements of culture. Role models are the people who demonstrate what success looks like within the plant. I am sure you know which people at your plant Mike favored. These were the ones who did whatever Mike asked and who were able to make the quickest repairs to the equipment. Of course, as a result of their actions, Mike rewarded them, or at least he didn't berate them as he did everyone else. As a result of their actions and Mike's reactions, others

embraced the "break it / fix it"
approach as a way to act and,
they hoped, to succeed. Those
who didn't were pushed out of
the way. The bottom line is that
Mike's culture was reinforced.
To change the culture you will
need new role models. You will
need people who model reliability-based values. These people
will need to be rewarded; as a
result, they will become the new
generation of role models of the
new culture.

The third element is referred to
as **rites and rituals**. Rituals
are what we do as part of our
everyday jobs — the work tasks,
if you will. They can cover the
entire range of the maintenance
spectrum: from rapid repairs to
reliability-based repairs.
Rites are how we reinforce the
rituals so that they continue.
To clarify the difference, work
planning and scheduling are rituals, and the reward for a job
well done is the rite. To change
your culture, both must be
changed and changed forever. Any
regression will undermine your
effort because you will be doing
the wrong things. Worse, you
will be reinforcing the wrong
behaviors.

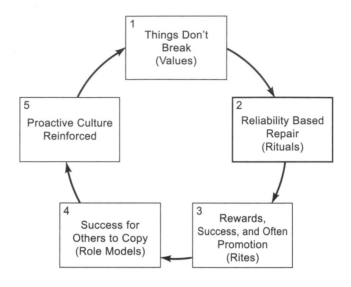

Let me show you a diagram of how
these three elements fit together within the new culture that
you are working to create.
Think of this model as the culture you are trying to change.
In Block #1, through your vision
and other tools, you establish a
new set of values. Then when
things do fail in Block #2, new
and different sets of rituals
are employed, ones based on
reliability-focused repairs. The
results for behaving in this new
fashion are rewards for those in
compliance — Block #3. People
see the rewards flowing to those
who follow the new set of values. New role models emerge in

Block #4, which in turn rein-
forces new values in Block #5.
You can use this as a roadmap.
It may prove helpful as you try
to explain organizational culture and how to change it.

The last of the four elements of
culture is somewhat different.
It is a set of behaviors that
you need to monitor if you are
going to protect and nurture the
change you are putting into
place. Failure to address this
element, which I call the cultural infrastructure, is a serious mistake. The primary role of
the **cultural infrastructure** is
to protect the culture that
exists. There are seven parts.

  1. Story Tellers. These are the
people who tell what most people
refer to as "war stories." When
you have heard these in the past
you probably thought that the
people telling the stories were
just wasting your time. Not so!
They were indirectly explaining
what the culture rewarded or
what behaviors it punished. You
need to build new stories pro-
moting the new culture and give
these people something constructive to do to support the change
effort.

2. Keepers of the Faith. People who fill this role are the organization's mentors. They teach others in the organization the correct way to work within the existing culture. Their lessons describe what someone must do to be successful. You need to engage these people so that they will mentor the new culture, not the old.

3. Gossips. Those who fill this role spread information and often the wrong information. If you don't communicate well, they will fill the voids, often causing you problems, setbacks, and the need to spend your time doing damage control. Remember the sixth element of change: communication. If you take the time to communicate well, you will mitigate any potential problems that could be caused by the gossips.

4. Spies. Passing information that you do not want disseminated is what spies do best. Whereas gossips spread rumors, spies pass along very specific information that is often incomplete or out of context. They can cause you and your change initiative serious problems. The damage that these individuals do can be eliminated through the same high level of communication that you use to handle the gossips. After all, if people are informed, then misinformation will be recognized and dismissed.

5. **Whisperers.** These people are the ones who pass information directly to senior managers, bypassing the normal communication processes. They are typically administrators who have contact with the upper levels of the organization's hierarchy on a frequent basis, as well as with the lower levels where the actual work is taking place. They can cause teams problems by once again sending the wrong or incomplete information. Knowing this as one of the leaders for this initiative can serve you well. Don't believe the things that the whisperers tell you without substantiating the information with facts. Assume nothing; validate everything, and it will keep you out of trouble.

6. **Symbols.** These are not people, but indicators of how we characterize or differentiate people and groups. For example, a large office, a reserved parking space, or even deferential treatment are symbols that show

the organization who is "in" and who is "out." When you eventually organize teams as part of your change effort, be careful of symbols that might undermine the effort. For example, giving team leaders better or bigger offices could serve to break down a cohesive team structure.

7. Language. The last part of cultural infrastructure is language, and I am referring specifically to the use of acronyms. If you have a meeting, make sure everyone present understands the language — the acronyms in use. Failure to do so sets up two groups: those who understand what is being said and those who do not. Because communication is so important, having people not understand what you are saying can hurt the change effort.

Todd, I know that this is a lot of material, but it is important that you understand it and address it as part of the process you are about to undertake. Have fun at your meeting.

I sat back trying to digest everything TAN had just told me. After thinking about it for a while, I began to see why change was so difficult and why change initiatives that only addressed hard skills were headed down the path to failure.

I had a lot to tell Pat if we were going to properly communicate the vision to the workforce tomorrow. I recognized from my dialogue with TAN that we had made a good start. However, we had a lot still to address. By the time I had organized my thoughts, it was getting late. The trouble was that I could not go home yet. Pat and I needed to plan for the communication meeting. We couldn't ad lib it; the meeting was just too important. So I called Pat on the phone.

"Pat, I know it's late but we need a much more definitive game plan for tomorrow's meeting. We need to do more than just hand out copies of the vision and read it to the organization. If we do only that, we will accomplish nothing, and we may be hurting the effort as well." I couldn't even begin to describe everything I had learned from TAN. Certainly I couldn't tell Pat about the e-mails. I suspected that he really didn't know what to do next. I was actually hoping that Pat would let me develop the presentation material that was needed for the meeting. I was in luck.

"Todd, I can't stay late tonight. It's my twenty-fifth wedding anniversary and I made plans to go out to dinner with my wife and kids. Could you just throw something together for review in the morning? We can meet first thing and go over it."

"No problem, Pat. I'll take care of it. I'll meet you in your office at 8 o'clock tomorrow morning. That will give us plenty of time to review your part of the presentation before the meeting. I just need to know that you are committed to this 100%."

"I'm with you Todd. I know we don't have a lot of time to get this right and I am sorry that I can't be available tonight, but I am certain that Mike's way won't work. We have to change. See you at 8:00."

So I called Susan and explained why I had to stay late. As always, she understood and told me that she knew I would succeed. Her words were the best energizer I could have received; after I hung up, I prepared for a very long night. I had made up my mind that more than the vision would take shape before I was done.

One other thing kept nagging at the back of my brain as I was preparing for the evening's work. It was the mysterious TAN and my ongoing e-mail discussions about implementing a change process at the Eastern Plant. I had asked numerous times in my e-mails who TAN actually was, but I never received an acknowledgement. I had spoken about the e-mails to Susan. At first I was reluctant to bring up the topic, but she didn't think I was totally crazy when I finally told her.

In fact, Susan told me that several years ago a friend of hers who was receiving strange e-mails had hired an agency to identify the sender. The internet detective service discovered the source and Susan's friend stopped receiving the unsolicited e-mails. In my case, the e-mails were helping, but I still wanted to know who was sending them. Meanwhile, Susan had contacted her friend and obtained the name of the agency. It was called ATIDA, short for Allie Thompson Internet Detective Agency. I wrote the number down and promised myself that as soon as I got an opportunity, I would unmask TAN.

CHAPTER 5

THE MEETING

At exactly 8 o'clock the next morning I was in Pat's office. I knew he would be there in a few minutes because I saw him pulling into the parking lot as I made my way up the glass-enclosed staircase to the second floor. I was tired. I had yesterday's beard because I never did get home last night. I had worked until 3 AM developing our approach and what we were going to say to the workforce. By the time I was done, I was just too tired to drive, so I went to sleep on the couch in my office. The one highlight of the evening was when Susan showed up with dinner. She was able to tell from my voice during our afternoon discussion that the task was going to be an all-night job. Dinner was great and her support of what I was trying to do even greater.

Pat seemed happy following what must have been a really nice anniversary dinner. That was until he saw me and recognized what I had done the previous evening. My appearance launched him into a round of profound apologies for not being there to help me. I made light of it, telling him that apologies were not needed. What we did need was success for our effort. After all, I had wanted to make these changes all along, but I needed Pat's involvement and commitment to make the effort a success. A little guilt on Pat's part might inspire the extra energy to make the effort work.

"Pat, we have a lot to discuss before the meeting. I have Lois setting everything up as far as the meeting logistics go. I even have her renting chairs so that there will be enough seating." (Our plant meeting area was big enough to accommodate everyone, but didn't have the seats.) "I have also had copies made of our vision. On the reverse side, I have taken the liberty of printing the meeting agenda. I took your direction and have the agenda here for your review." There wasn't much he was going to do to change it since I already was having the copies made. "I also have taken the liberty of putting on paper some opening remarks. After all, you are now the plant manager and it is important that you kick off the meeting. The people need to see you as their new leader and that you are committed to our new direction."

I had prepared well, so I showed Pat the agenda.

The New ATP3Co Meeting Agenda

Opening remarks	Pat Collingwood
The Vision for the new ATP3Co	Todd Bradley
How we are going to achieve the vision	Todd Bradley
Questions	Todd Bradley
Next steps start now	Todd Bradley

He looked it over. I knew he was going to have questions and I was ready. I had spent the whole night getting ready.

"Todd, I have two questions. First what is the '3' doing in the company name?"

"That's easy! Remember the vision we created? Under Mike, the 'P' in ATPCo was for production and you see where that got us. Under the new ATP3Co, we are going to use our vision statement to redefine the 'P' to include production, performance, and people. I want everyone to see a new picture of our plant in their mind's eye when they think about our business. And I want everyone to remember the vision. Of course, they won't remember all of the words, but the three 'P's are going to stick and be remembered by everyone."

"The next item is somewhat trickier," Pat said. "I'm not a good public speaker. In fact, I am scared to death to get up in front of the workforce and make even the simplest speech."

Once again I was ready. I knew from past experience that Pat didn't like to make speeches. "Pat it's no problem. I have written out your speech for you. In fact, I have prepared it on sheets of paper with oversized fonts so standing at the podium you can almost read it and still appear to the audience as if you are not. It is often how the politicians make speeches. All we need to do is to rehearse it a few times and you will be fine. Let me show you what I wrote," I said as I handed him the speech.

Pat's Speech

"Good afternoon. I want to welcome you to the first and, I promise, not the last communication meeting for the Eastern Plant. Most of you know me, but for those who don't, my name is Pat Collingwood. I started working here when the plant was built and have worked as an operator, a supervisor, and recently as production manager. Then just a few days ago several significant things happened. First, Mike Kane had a massive heart attack and died — a very sad day for all of us. That you know.

"What you may or may not know is the second item. A new formulation has been discovered for tractium. It is called Epsilon. It can be produced with the equipment we have here in the plant with some modifications to the line. The result is a much more diverse product with very great profit potential. Not only that, but the geographical center of the new market for Epsilon is right here in the east. Consider both the way we are set up as a company, and the high costs and reduced profit if we try to ship from our other sites. Given those considerations, we either deliver Epsilon to our customers here in the east or ATPCo doesn't get into the Epsilon business. The latter would have a huge negative financial impact for the company as well as devastating implications for all of us here today.

"Furthermore, a new customer is considering us as a supplier of Epsilon. In less than three months, they are planning to visit the Eastern Plant to determine if we are a company they want as one of their suppliers. We want, we need this contract.

"Allen Peters, our president, has asked me to fill in as temporary plant manager and to do whatever is needed to position us to get the Epsilon business. I can tell you with great certainty that if we were visited today, the customer would walk away in disgust. Our equipment is unreliable and is shut down more often than running. All we know how to do is to respond to the Line Down alarm that Mike had installed and fix things quickly with no regard to long-term reliability. We need to change and to change quickly!

"Under Mike, the 'P' in ATPCo stood only for production. Production at all cost, even if we were just putting patches on the problems and never really addressing the real reliability issues. Well, that stops here and now. Mike is gone and so is his management style. From today onward, ATPCo is going to have three 'P's, just as it shows on the agenda. They will stand for production, performance, and most of all people.

"Now I don't ask any of you to believe my words. You have probably heard similar words before. You probably expect to leave here and within a few days have the plant under Pat be the same as the plant was under Mike. No, I don't expect you to believe what I say. What I do expect is that we work together and make the three 'P's of

ATPCo a reality. What I want from each of
you is to look at and believe my actions in
support of what I have just said. I also
expect you to tell me and my staff if we fall
short, with absolutely no fear of punishment
because there won't be any. We need to
know what we are doing right and what we
are doing wrong. And we don't have a lot of
time to do it right if we want that Epsilon
contract.

"Standing next to me is Todd Bradley, your
maintenance manager for the last six
months. Todd is going to lead this effort to
achieve the three 'P's of ATPCo. I said lead
because Todd can not accomplish the
change alone. Your active involvement is
critical to our ultimate success. Together we
can not only win the Epsilon contract, but
also we can become the best plant in the
business!

"Ladies and gentlemen — welcome to the
new ATPCo and the first day of the rest of
your lives. Thank you, and here's Todd."

Pat sat back and said, "Todd this is really good
material. I almost believe it myself."

When I heard these words from Pat, a warning
alarm sounded in my head. I remembered what TAN had
told me about leadership. The leaders set the vision. But
even more important, they convey and reinforce the
organizational values. If we had any hope of succeeding,
then Pat had to do more than believe. He had to sell that
belief to everyone. He also had to practice what he
preached, as I told him in no uncertain terms.

"Pat, if you don't believe that we can achieve the

vision, then everyone will know that you are not committed to accomplishing the words coming out of your mouth," I said. "Pat, this is the real deal. Either we change and improve our operation now or we all are finished. Our competition will change in order to produce Epsilon and we must change as well. We need to run the plant reliably. You know Mike's way didn't work. We need to know why our equipment fails and correct the root of the problem, not just patch it up and go back on line until it fails again."

The discussion went on for two hours, which is why I started it at eight. I needed not only to have Pat ready, but also to have him truly believe so that what he delivered was more than just a speech; it was his commitment to change. By 11 o'clock Pat was ready. Moreover, I firmly believed that he was committed to making a change at the plant.

As we stepped into the meeting hall and walked to the podium, I could tell that everyone in the plant was present. We had scheduled the meeting at lunch because it was a good time to get the entire organization together. When I say everyone, I meant it. Pat and I had agreed, after a lot of hot debate, to shut down the lines so that everyone could attend. Fortunately shutting down a line and then restarting it safely was not a major problem. The operators could restart the equipment after the meeting and quickly be back on line. After all, as I had explained to Pat when making my case, the lines would each be down at some point during the day anyway as a result of some failure, so what really was the issue?

I stepped up to the microphone and called the meeting to order. As soon as everyone had settled down and taken their seats, I introduced Pat and he stepped to the microphone. I must admit our rehearsals had done wonders, not only for his confidence but also for his delivery. Having the speech in large font also helped him appear as if he was simply speaking and not reading the material. Before long, he completed his speech. There was a round of applause, but I could tell we did not yet have support of the audience. After all, until a few days ago, these people had all lived under the yoke of Mike Kane. Why should they believe things were going to change? It was as Pat had said, "you need to wait and believe in my actions, not simply my words."

Then it was my turn. "Thanks, Pat. I can tell from the looks on your faces that you are skeptical about the things that Pat has said. No doubt you have seen and heard other managers telling you how things were going to be different. Worse, in your most recent experience you were continually told that you were worthless and that the only reason you were here to do was to get tractium out the door. It was 'Mike's way or the highway.' I mean no disrespect to Mike or his memory, but his way didn't work. Starting today we are going to change things. We, all of us, are embarking on a journey to make things better for our company and for all of us as well.

"One thing I know for sure, and that is if you want to know where you are going, you need a vision of the future. Without a clear vision that is shared and understood by everyone, you wind up doing the same old things the same old way and — guess what — you always get the same old results. That's bad enough, but in addition to that you most likely never know why.

"Here at the Eastern Plant, we are going to change all of that. The day after Mike died, I talked with many of you about what you thought our vision of the future should be. From those discussions, I received a lot of valuable input. From all of that information, Pat and I came up with the idea of ATPCo having not one but three 'P's in the name. We also developed a vision, which is printed on the other side of your handout. Let me read it to you:

> *"We will operate our plant so that equipment never fails in a unplanned fashion. This high level of reliability will enable us to continuously supply the demand of our customers as well as take on new ones. We will perform this work in a way that recognizes the important and unique value that each person brings to the effort.*

"I don't expect you to remember this statement word for word. You have copies, but still I don't expect it to be remembered. What I do want is for you to remember the three 'P's. The 'P' in ATPCo doesn't just stand for production any longer. It now stands for production, performance, and people — our three keys to a successful operation. Keep them in mind because this is how we are going to operate from now on.

"A vision however is not enough. There is a foundation upon which change is built; it is called the soft skill level. Another way to look at what this foundation means to us is by examining the components that make up soft skills. These components are called the eight elements of change. Let me briefly tell you about each because they are very important if we are going to successfully change things around.

"The first is leadership. Leaders set the direction. The problem is that when you and I think of leaders, we visualize people like Allen, Mike, or even Pat. True, these people are leaders, but I need to tell you that each and every one of you is a leader (or can be) in your own way. The operators can lead the way to reliable production. Maintenance can lead the way by doing the work in a well-planned, reliability-focused fashion. Others can lead the way within their own functions. All of us can, in fact, all of us must, become these leaders of change. How this will take shape may not be very clear to you today. But as we move forward, you will see your leadership roles emerge and become reality.

"The second element is work process, or how things get done around here. All of you know the reactive manner in which work was accomplished under Mike, but that is going to change. We are going to focus on the reliability of our equipment. If something breaks down, we are not going to quickly patch it up just to get back on line. We are going to shut it down safely, take it apart carefully, and find out why it failed. There are techniques to do this and all of you are going to learn to become reliability thinkers.

Then, when we figure out why the equipment failed, we are going to fix it so that it never fails again – just like our vision says. This approach will have more meaning for you in the weeks to come. But for now, when a line goes down, we will fix it right. No more "fast fix" so it can break down again tomorrow. We can't run our existing lines that way and we certainly can't produce Epsilon that way either.

"Along with the work process changes, we are going to develop a revised organizational structure. Under Mike, Production and Maintenance did not operate in harmony. There were and still are many barriers to getting the job done. Of course, Maintenance will still be responsible for equipment repairs. Now, however, everyone else is going to be trained so that they understand not just how to operate the equipment, but also how to take care of the equipment so it keeps operating.

"The fourth element is group learning. To get better, we need to learn from each other and apply what we learn to the business. This element of change is extraordinarily important. Under Mike, the environment was my way or, well, you all know the rest. Yet ATPCo hasn't hired you just to do what people tell you, working basically from the neck down. No, we hired you to think and help us get better. We need what's above your shoulders as well. We need, no, we expect, your ideas on any subject. After all, many of you know this operation far better than Pat or I do. No subject is off limits. No subject is closed. You may not like the answer or even the outcome of some decisions, but you will have your idea considered and get feedback.

"Communication and interrelationships are the next two elements. Communication starts here and now. No more speculation about what is going on, what we plan, or the challenges before us. A good example of improved communication is the information we provided you about the Epsilon contract. We plan to have other meetings of this sort and share our plans. In the future, it won't just be Pat or I who are speaking. You will hear from others, many of whom may be your peers. This communication and other activities will help build solid interrelationships across our plant. With the current state of the operation, it is essential that all of us pull together in the same direction. As Ben Franklin once said, 'We must all hang together, or assuredly we shall all hang separately.' My plan is for us to hang together — but definitely not in the literal sense!

"The last of the eight elements is rewards. What are the rewards for all of the work we are about to undertake? More money? I see a lot of heads nodding to that answer! I wish, and although that may be what first comes to mind, there actually are better rewards. First is our ability to have jobs and make a decent wage. I'd rather have that for years than a few thousand dollars for a year. Now I'm sure that many of you feel that ATPCo has been here for twenty-five years and will be here at least twenty-five more, regardless of what we do. However, look at other companies that no longer exist. You will quickly realize that your confidence could be a wrong assumption. With Epsilon on the market, and specifically in our geographic area, we could lose the new contract without a reliably operating plant. I for one will be thinking about another job if we can't address the Epsilon market. Therefore, one of our key rewards is continuity.

"The second reward, one that I think is equally important, is to be able to come to work each day and enjoy it. You don't need to raise your hands, but how many of you enjoyed working under Mike? In that regard, you can see there are rather significant rewards out there for all of us if we succeed.

"So, there you have it — the eight elements of change and how they impact each and every one of us here at ATPCo. What we are promising you is that there is going to be change, and it will be for the better. Not just better for ATPCo, not just better for management, but better for us all. Thank you. I will now open up to the floor for questions. Remember: there is no punishment for asking. The real punishment is not asking your question and leaving here without the answer."

Gene Smith, the union president, raised his hand. He was sitting in the front row. Getting a portable microphone to him so everyone could hear what he was going to say was easy for Lois, who had volunteered for the task.

Gene cleared his throat. I was on pins and needles because I didn't know what he was going to say. I just hoped it was in some way supportive of the initiative we were trying to implement. "Pat, Todd, we have been living in what I would call very frustrating times. The rank and file know maybe even better than you what needs to be done. Mike wouldn't let us do anything to make this place better. I guess he felt if he yelled and threatened everyone long and hard enough that things would improve. Of course they didn't.

"I listened to all of the things that you and Pat have said here today. While I still want proof, what you are offering seems to be far better than the way things were in the past. That said, the union will support you. But, as I said when we met on the shop floor the other day, we are taking a leap of faith. Don't let us down."

Gene's statement seemed to lighten the atmosphere in the room considerably, but I wasn't about to let Gene off of the hook so easily. "Gene," I said. "Thank you for your support, but I want more than just words from you as well. I need your involvement in the effort. We are forming a steering team to oversee and provide guidance to the process. I want you to become an active member. You have been here a long time. You know the people and, as you just said, you know what needs to be done. If we are going to make this place better, we need your help. What do you say?"

Of course, Gene accepted a long, resounding

applause from the assembled group. Many other questions followed. We spent about forty-five minutes answering them. At last, everyone seemed satisfied and I could tell from the restlessness of the audience that they were ready to go back to work. But I wasn't done yet. I had not talked about the next steps. So I got up and went back to the podium. Everyone thought that I was going to end the meeting and they all started to get up. "Hold on a few more minutes," I said to the group. "We aren't exactly done yet. If you leave now, then in a day or so this gathering is just going to seem like one more meeting with a lot of talk and no action. Let me tell you two things that are going to take place today.

"First, right after lunch, the Line Down alarm will be disabled and removed. We aren't going to need it any more. Second, coming onto the stage is someone you don't know. His name is Fred Baxter and he owns Consolidated Radio. 'How does he have anything to do with our effort,' you may ask. Well at the end of this meeting I want all managers, maintenance foremen, and lead operators to come up to the stage and get a radio. From here on out, if the line goes down, production is to contact me, the area maintenance foreman, and engineering. Then they are to make the line safe for work, but touch nothing. Before we do any work to restore operation, I will coordinate a response that will focus on finding out exactly what went wrong and why. We are going to start fixing equipment so that it doesn't break. Remember the three 'P's, one of which is performance. Well, that is it for now. Our target from here on out is reliable operation. Again, thank you for your attendance today and welcome to the new ATP3Co."

With that, everyone filed out while all those mentioned in my closing remarks came to the stage to receive their radios. Pat and I returned to his office, each of us physically and emotionally drained. We had started down a new road with what we both believed was a successful meeting. As we ate a very late lunch, we listened to everyone playing with their new radios. To an outside observer, it might have seemed funny, but I knew it was a first step to improved communication.

CHAPTER 6

THE STEERING TEAM

In Pat's office following the meeting, I was feeling quite good about the outcome. Still, I was waiting to see Pat's reaction, especially since he had not had much involvement in its development. Yes, it was true that his speech was a central part of the meeting, but I had written it and rehearsed him until I felt he had it right. And I needed more than his words. Whether he liked it or not, he was the plant manager and needed to set the direction. If he didn't believe in all that he said and all that I had set in motion, then all would be lost even before we got started. After all, as TAN had said, a great many people can be leaders, but the person at the top is the ultimate leader. That person must set and sustain the values and the vision. All of us needed Pat to do that so that we could change from the poorly-operating plant we were to one that was reliable and could secure the Epsilon contract.

Pat was all smiles. "Todd, I think we've done it."

"Done what?" I really wanted to see what he meant and hoped that he didn't think we had solved all of the plant's problems with one meeting.

"You know, started the change in motion. All we need to do now is figure out what's next. I know we don't have all of the answers yet, but I feel a lot more hopeful than I have for the last few days."

"Pat, I agree with you. I think we have made an excellent start, but the real work hasn't even begun. The organization is looking for change. They know we are having serious reliability problems. They know about Epsilon and the potential contract that will either make us or break us. What we gave them today was basically two important things. First we gave them a vision of a far different future than the one they have experienced under Mike's rule. Second we gave them hope that we were going to help them get better.

Although these are two really good ways to get things started, we now need to deliver. The radios, the disabling and removal of the Line Down alarm, and taking the time to analyze our equipment failures before we restart a line are still concepts until we actually show everyone how they add value. Also, don't forget, we don't have a lot of time to convert at least one line to Epsilon production and demonstrate reliable operation when our future customer visits."

I could see that I had somewhat burst Pat's bubble. I guess he believed that telling people that things were going to change would somehow magically make it all happen. Now he was beginning to realize that there was far more to making the change successful than he had originally thought.

"So what's next? How do we build on what we started today?" Pat said with the excitement returning to his voice.

I hadn't stayed up and gone without sleep these last few nights for nothing. I already had developed an answer to this question, which I had hoped that Pat would ask. True, I didn't have the whole answer, but at least I had the initial part. "Pat, we need to create and drive all future changes using a team approach. Using teams will support many, if not all, of the eight elements of change and help us with the four elements of culture.

To start, we need a steering team. This group would include you, me, Gene, and some others who would set direction and provide overall guidance for the organization. If we are truly going to achieve our vision, then we need guidance from a balanced group who can provide it and hold the rest of the organization accountable to achieve it. One of the first things this group can do is to help us figure out how to get one of the lines converted to reliably producing Epsilon."

Pat liked the idea of a steering team. I think I had convinced him on the basis of some of the eight elements of change. After all, we were bringing leadership, communication, interrelationships, and even rewards into the process. I also think that Pat convinced himself simply because he didn't know where to start and having other people's ideas in the mix would deliver a better solution.

One problem: I personally liked the idea of a steering team, which is why I had suggested it. However, I really didn't know exactly how to go about setting it up or the details involved. I suspected that once we assembled the team we could figure it out by trial and error. Nevertheless, there had to be a better way than false starts and team frustration from lack of a clear direction.

Pat and I sat in his office for about another half hour. We had both brought lunch so while we ate we discussed both who should be on the steering team and the content for the first meeting's agenda. We agreed that the key members of Pat's staff along with Gene Smith, the union president, would be core members. I also suggested, and Pat agreed, that one hourly operator and one mechanic would also be part of the team. Pat had initially balked at this idea until I described the cultural infrastructure. I wanted hourly representation so that the workforce would recognize the effort was not solely being handled by management. I also needed people from the workforce who would allow us to address concerns about the Keepers of the Faith, Storytellers, and Gossips. I knew that one of our goals was to create a reliability-focused work culture. From what TAN had told me, and from what I knew on my own, the hourly people I had in mind would help me address the cultural infrastructure issues. So at the end of our meeting, we had our recommended steering team:

Pat Collingwood	Plant Manager
Pete Jackson	Production Manager
Sally Franks	Engineering Manager
Todd Bradley	Maintenance / ReliabilityManager
Nick Landis	Senior Maintenance Mechanic
Dani Sommers	Operator – Line #1
Gene Smith	Union President
Lois Lang	Pat's administrative assistant

Nick Landis and Dani Sommers were people who I had carefully selected. First, they would bring balance to the group because they were both highly respected in the maintenance and operations areas respectively. Second, I wanted them to help me to tackle the cultural infrastructure issues needed if our efforts were to be successful.

Nick had worked at the eastern plant for twenty-five years. He was hired as a line mechanic apprentice and had then helped build the four product lines that were currently operating. He was also one of the key people who kept the lines running even in their poorly-maintained state. He knew all there was to know about maintaining the equipment. Additionally he was the mentor (Keeper of the Faith) for the entire maintenance organization. That meant that under Mike he was the best "rapid repair" mechanic we had on staff. My job was to convert him and have him take on the role of the keeper of the new reliability faith. This task would not be an easy one, but I believed converting Nick was essential to our overall success.

Dani Sommers was a different case. Over the past ten years she had proven time and time again to be one of the best operators in the company. She was so good that she had advanced to lead operator, passing others on the line who had greater seniority.

She had other qualifications as well that would make her a valuable asset to the steering team. She operated Line #1, which was the line we were going to convert to the production of Epsilon. She was also, in my estimation, the biggest gossip in the plant. This attribute meant that she could have quite an impact on the cultural infrastructure. I had plans to utilize this trait as a positive communication conduit to the organization. I concluded that it was better to have accurate communication going through the gossip process than to have the organization speculate, potentially drawing wrong conclusions about what we were doing, and causing us to lose time by having to conduct continuous damage control. We had no time for damage control; it needed to be avoided.

Lois Lang, Pat's administrative assistant, was actually Pat's idea since he wanted someone who could take accurate meeting notes. I heartily agreed but for a far different reason. She was also an important part of the cultural infrastructure. She was a whisperer — a person in the organization who others used to pass information to the boss without going through channels. I had known that she occupied this role for a long time, but didn't put a label on her actions until TAN identified the role she filled. There was no other way that Mike could have known all of the things he knew. I concluded that Lois's trait of passing information would be of value as we moved forward.

Pat and I set up the steering team meeting for 9:00 AM on Monday; Pat had Lois send out the announcement. Lois was both pleased and surprised when Pat told her of her new role. It was her idea not only to e-mail invitations to the team but also to contact them personally so that all members would understand the importance of their attendance at the meeting.

Back at the office I closed the door and e-mailed TAN explaining what had happened at the meeting and how we planned to proceed. I even included copies of both Pat's speech and my own so that TAN could read what we had said. I further explained about the steering team and, although I don't like to admit it, asked for suggestions for our next steps. TAN's response was quick — within the hour. I almost suspected that he was waiting for my e-mail.

 To: Todd Bradley
From: TAN

It looks like you are on the correct path. You and Pat said a lot of good things in your communications meeting. Now it is time to act on your words. Otherwise, your words are hollow. The steering team is a good idea and can help set the direction for the plant. I also like the way you addressed some of the cultural infrastructure elements. You really were paying attention to my e-mail about culture!

Now you need to know more about teams. You might think that a steering team will deliver all that you need. I hope you don't actually believe that because if you do, you are wrong. Here is some additional information that may help as you proceed.

First let's define what a team is. In their book The Wisdom of Teams (New York: Harper, 1994), Jon R. Katzenbach and Douglas K. Smith define teams as follows:

"A team is a small number of people with complementary skills who are committed to a common purpose, performance goals and approach for which they hold themselves mutually accountable."

Think about how this definition relates to the steering team you will be forming tomorrow morning and answer these questions:

1. Is the group the right size (minimum 4 - maximum 12)?
2. Do the members possess complementary (supporting)skills?
3. Are they committed to a common purpose?
4. Do they have common performance goals?
5. Do they have a common approach to the effort?
6. Do they hold themselves mutually accountable?

> Todd, write out the answers to
> these questions and send them to
> me. If you answer yes, then why?
> If you answer no, why not and
> what are you going to do to cor-
> rect the problem? Consider this
> to be a homework assignment. If
> you want help for tomorrow's
> meeting, complete this assign-
> ment as soon as possible!

I have to admit that Pat and I had not addressed these questions, let alone developed an appropriate course of action for building an effective and efficient steering team. Actually, until I saw TAN's e-mail, I had never considered the details associated with building a properly-functioning team. If we were going to build a well functioning steering team, I needed to think about and answer TAN's questions. It didn't take me very long.

To: TAN
From: Todd Bradley

1. Is the group the right size
   (minimum 4 - maximum 12)?
We have eight people, so we are
in the correct range for an
effective team.
2. Do they possess complementary
   (supporting) skills?
I believe that the people have
complementary skills. The team
includes the managers of the key
business areas and line repre-

sentatives from both maintenance
and production. We also included
the union president. As much as
anyone, he wants our efforts to
be successful. Having him on the
team firms up that commitment as
well as providing another communication conduit to the workforce.
3. Are they committed to a common purpose?
Not right now. They understand
the need to make changes, or at
least I think they do. However,
we haven't yet met so I suspect
they have not given any thought
to what it means to be individually or collectively committed.
I hope that working through all
of the tasks required to make
the changes we need will achieve
this end.
4. Do they have common performance goals?
Not yet. We will be setting
goals at our first meeting. I
think our goals will need more
clarification and more preci-
sion. But I wanted to get
through the first meeting before
I asked. Just getting organized
may be challenging enough for a
first task.
5. Do they have a common
approach   to the effort?
No. We will develop this as we

go along. I am sure that I will
have questions about this item as
well after the team meets.
6. Do they hold themselves mutually accountable?
Again, no. I am not even sure how
to accomplish this aspect of
working with a team. After the
first meeting, I hope I will have
a clearer sense of how to proceed. Of course, your recommendations would be welcome.

I hit the send bar and sat back, fairly depressed. I
had answered "no" or "I don't know" to four of the six
questions defining a team. I had thought that team building was going to be easier than it was turning out to be.
However, I am not by nature a defeatist. There was too
much at stake to fail, so I tried to refocus on how I was
going to achieve success. With a large cup of coffee and
my door closed to avoid disturbances, I began to think
about my four "no" answers. It dawned on me that I could
structure our meeting agenda to address these questions
as well as others that were sure to arise at the meeting.
This agenda would help the group recognize and work
through the same issues that, once resolved, would help
them become a team. Then, before I could proceed, a new
e-mail arrived from TAN.

 To: Todd Bradley
From: TAN

Surprise! Building a team is
harder than you thought. Four out
of six is not very good. You have

a lot of preparation ahead of
you for tomorrow's meeting.
Consider answering the four "no"
questions as part of your agenda. Let me know how the meeting
works out.

When I read the e-mail, a smile crossed my face.
The direction TAN had provided was the same one I had
developed all by myself. What fantastic reinforcement,
and with that I got to work. A few hours later and a trash
can filled with false starts, I had finished the agenda
along with a strategy to address the questions that made
up the definition of a team. Here is what the agenda
looked like:

Steering Team Agenda
  1. Introductions
  2. Review of the current issues
  3. Why you were selected
  4. Finalizing the vision
  5. Defining our goals
  6. How we will approach the process
  7. Our responsibilities to ourselves and each
     other
  8. Close

On Monday at exactly 9:00 AM, everyone assembled in the conference room to begin the first meeting of
the steering team. Pat opened the meeting with some
welcoming comments and thanked everyone for attending. He then turned the meeting over to me, mentioning
once again that I was going to lead the effort. I also

thanked everyone for attending, then handed out and briefly reviewed the contents of the agenda. The review of the current issues wasn't all that difficult because everyone already knew what they were from the previous day's communication meeting, but I listed them on a flip chart anyway.

* Our equipment is unreliable
* We can not deliver per our customer's demands
* We have already lost several contracts because of bullets #1 and #2
* Our plant personnel need a reliability focus breaking the old rapid-repair model
* We need to start producing Epsilon to compete in the new market
* We are being reviewed by a potential Epsilon customer in less than 90 days
* We need to achieve long-term improvement, which means instituting a culture change embracing the three Ps (production, performance, and people)

I wanted to jump right into solving the problem, but I stayed with the agenda. After all, this was not a short-term project; it was a long-term process change and needed to be treated as such.

The next part of the discussion was to explain to the group why each of the members was selected. Of course, I mentioned that Pat and I considered each of them strong leaders for various reasons that I explained in depth. I also stressed the various skills that each one brought to the team. I wanted them to recognize the complementary skills that each provided and to understand how powerful the group would be when these skills were combined. As I spoke, I could see from the group's facial expressions that they had some understanding of why they had been selected. I also saw determination because they all knew the problems we faced and the rewards if we were able to overcome those problems.

Next on the agenda was the review of the vision. We had presented it at the communication meeting the prior day so everyone had time to think about its meaning. Pat and I answered a few questions, but for now, no one wanted to change it. Still, as a group, we agreed to review it as our plans for changing the culture evolved. In that way, the vision would be somewhat "evergreen." Although we didn't want to alter the ultimate picture of our future state, we did want to be able to improve upon it later. The one thing that everyone liked was the three-"P" concept. We agreed to think about ways to embed this concept in the workforce as the true vision of the plant.

The effort so far had only taken about an hour, but now the fun was about to begin. I wasn't sure what our goals should be. Frankly, if asked to define what "goals" themselves were, I would be hard pressed to provide a definition. Nevertheless, we decided to list all of the items that we as a team believed were goals for this effort. To assemble this list, we used a "brainstorming" technique that I had used in the past. The process involved going around the room with each person providing a goal until we had exhausted our ideas. When a person's turn came, he or she could add an item to the list or pass. An important part of brainstorming was that no one was allowed to comment on another person's idea. The plan was to make the list first, then do the analysis later. So we started making our list and I wrote each one down on the flip chart. Here is what the team listed:

- Become more reliable
- Treat people with dignity and respect
- Convert Line #1 to Epsilon production
- Bring our equipment back to design
- Find out why equipment fails and correct it forever
- Win the Epsilon contract / pass the review
- Stay in business
- No unplanned line shutdowns
- Develop a preventive and predictive maintenance program
- Improve our repair process
- Institute the three "P"s
- Better treatment of operators
- Change to a better way of working and make it stick
- Eliminate the rapid repair process
- Include reliability engineers in the repair process
- Expand team membership
- Employ teams throughout the plant

There were other items listed, but I have excluded them because they essentially duplicated others already on the list. In the end, everyone felt that they had an opportunity to list their items and when their next turn came they passed. Then an amazing thing happened. Everyone began talking at once, trying to promote their ideas over the ideas of others. If we hadn't been working to resolve a serious situation, it would have been comical to watch — people talking and not one person listening.

This apparent chaos was a good lead into our next topic: how we were going to work together to approach this process. "Everyone!" I called out. "Let's take a fifteen-minute break. Then when we return, let's not try to figure out our goals. Instead let's talk about the process we are going to follow and the rules we are going to live by as a team in order to accomplish our task." Thus, everyone stopped trying to sell their ideas and we took a break.

Breaks are not called just to allow people to get more coffee, answer phone messages, or go to the restroom. They also serve other important functions. Breaks allow you to interrupt the meeting so that people have time to think, reconsider positions, or even to meet off-line in smaller groups. They also provide the facilitator the ability to break up confrontation and participants to settle down after an emotional debate. I called this break for all of these reasons.

When we resumed, I told everyone we would return to the goals later, but I wanted to focus next on developing rules for team behavior. Someone, I don't remember who, asked about the necessity for this step. I simply reminded everyone of the state of the team before the break. With that picture clear in their minds, everyone quieted down and focused on the next step.

While everyone was out of the room, I had written a few rules on our flip chart. I entitled them Team Rules of Conduct. I have listed them below in no particular order:
- One person speaks at a time
- Eliminate idea destroyers ("we can't" – and others)
- Everyone's ideas have value
- Ask for clarification — don't assume
- Look to the future, not to the past
- Arrive at the meeting on time

- No interruptions during the meeting (cell phones off)
- Stay at the meeting — block out your schedule
- Silence is not acceptance — speak your mind
- Stay on topic — use the parking lot approach for items outside the discussion
- Decide by consensus
- Be open to new ideas — nothing is a given
- What is said here stays here
- No topic is off limits if the approach is constructive

I explained that the list was not comprehensive and asked for other ideas from the group. In fact, the last three items listed above are not mine; they came from Gene, Dani, and Pat. There was some discussion as we added the last three items. Nevertheless, no one had any significant issue with any of the items except I was asked to clarify the concept of consensus. This term confused many in the group who thought that all decisions had to be unanimous. I responded that if that were the case nothing would ever be decided because it is virtually impossible to get everyone to agree. Consensus, I explained, is one step short of unanimous agreement. With consensus, everyone may not totally agree, but they all are willing to agree that they can live with the decision or direction. This allows a team to bring the discussion of an issue to completion.

The next item on the agenda was the topic of our responsibilities to each other. Having read TAN's notes about the eight elements of change, I knew that this was number seven, interrelationships, but didn't say anything to the group for fear of confusing the effort. I knew, however, that if we were to be successful as a team our inter-relationships would be critical. The biggest hurdle that we needed to get past was Mike Kane and the management style he had fostered during his time as manager. All the people on the team, yes even the managers, had been told how to think and act for so long that they were finding it difficult and stressful to do any thinking for themselves. They were not yet ready to be mutually accountable, but they needed to start. My plan was to start them with our random list of goals. Obviously the items needed more development, so I directed the steering team to develop the details and prioritize the items. The ground rules were simple:

1. Write down your understanding of each item.
2. Work in sub-teams of two people: Pat and Nick, Pete and Dani, and Sally and Gene.
3. Have the work done by the next meeting, which was to be in two days — same time, same place.

I excluded myself from the sub-teams. I had other tasks to perform such as contacting TAN because I was about out of ideas. I also excluded Lois; instead I asked her to meet with each of the teams and summarize their notes for the review of the full team. Meanwhile, this assignment into sub-teams generated several questions and many concerns. I've listed some of the more interesting ones so you will have some insight into my strategy.

1. Why two days? We need more time than that to do all this work along with our regular jobs.
   Answer: From now on this is your regular job. Delegate the rest of your work as you see fit

> but, as Pat will confirm, this is job #1.
> 2.How did you pick the teams?
> *Answer: I wanted to mix line and staff. I want*
> *you to get to know your teammates better.*
> 3.What if our team needs more clarification
> about one of the goals. Will you provide the
> answer?
> *Answer: No I won't. I didn't create them. Ask*
> *members of the other teams what they think or,*
> *if you remember, the person who suggested the*
> *item.*
> 4.How are we going to consolidate the results?
> *Answer: I'll tell you at the next meeting.*
> *(I hoped TAN would help me with this one.)*

At this point we had been working for four hours and it was past lunch. I asked for any final questions or comments. Because there were none, I closed the meeting. On my way out, I almost walked into a small scaffold in the hall. The mechanics were removing the Line Down alarm, which had been disabled the day before. If there was a problem, I had my radio and I would be called. It wasn't a major step. But certainly coupled with the radios we had distributed, it was a visible indication to the plant personnel that change was underway.

The day had been stressful simply because I had not been sure how it was going to turn out. However, it had gone well. I was tired, not just from the stress but also from lack of sleep the prior two days. Even though I really wanted to go home and get some rest, I still had one more thing to do.

Not knowing TAN's identify was driving me crazy. Of course, I more than appreciated the advice and direction that he had provided so far. In fact I was beginning to rely heavily on TAN as a change management mentor; I hoped that his stream of information and direction would continue to support our change efforts. But still I needed to know who TAN actually was. Could I get to meet and work with him, not just communicate via e-mail? Therefore, I had called the number that Susan had given me, the Allie Thompson Internet Detective Agency (ATIDA), and had set up a meeting for 5 o'clock that evening. The office wasn't very far from the plant so at the end of the day I drove over.

ATIDA occupied a small, one-room office in an industrial park full of several identical buildings all containing small businesses. The office door was marked with the room number and a sign that read ATIDA, so it was easy to find. I wasn't sure that this undertaking was going to be worthwhile, but TAN had ignored all of my inquiries into his identity. Thus, until someone gave me another solution to my quest, ATIDA was my only choice.

Allie Thompson, the owner and as far as I could tell the sole employee, was sitting at her desk as I entered. She was young, but that was to be expected. It seems to me that I struggle with computers and their associated systems, while younger people are born with the skills. Therefore, youth to me in this type of business was no surprise. She also seemed to be very busy; her business must be lucrative, I thought. Her office was neat and from the looks of it well organized, but she had quite a number of files on her desk. I assumed all were clients.

As I was to find out, Allie was all business and got right to the point. "Todd, Allie Thompson. I know you are here to have me locate someone who has been sending you anonymous e-mails. Your case is somewhat different because, as you told me over the phone, you don't want the e-mails to stop. You just want to know who is sending them. Well, you're in the right place. I may look young, but I have a lot of experience and can give you numerous references. My fee is $1000 upfront and I will refund half if I am not successful. I also need to tell you that this may take months. My search will actually be determined by how difficult your mysterious TAN is to locate. I don't have time right now to explain the process; we can do that later if you wish. I will find TAN. Do we have a deal?"

Allie came straight to the point. I had not been in her office for ten minutes and she had already explained her services and asked if I planned to employ her. I liked her no-nonsense style and signed the contract that she had slid across her desk. We then spent another half hour going over the details of my interaction with TAN. As we got more comfortable, she explained that the abrupt introduction was to get rid of people who were not serious about having her do Internet detective work. She explained that with the volume of work she had, she had no time for people who were not serious. We discussed a few more minor points, I wrote her a check, and left with the assurance that I would hear from her in about one month. I hoped that my money had been well spent. For my own sake, I needed to unmask the mysterious TAN.

CHAPTER 7

THE GOAL ACHIEVEMENT MODEL

Following the steering team meeting, and before heading for home, I had sent TAN an e-mail describing our first meeting. I thought the meeting had gone very well. We had identified a set of goals and the sub-groups were working on defining each in greater detail. I was also pleased with myself for how I had formed the sub-teams. Knowing about the eight elements of change from TAN's prior e-mail had helped me to envision a way to improve communication and interrelationships, and to get more definition for our goal list all at the same time. I included the goal list in my e-mail, asking TAN if he had any comments. One other thing — I thanked TAN for the help he had provided thus far in the process because, quite honestly, much if not all of my inspiration had evolved from his previous e-mails.

As expected, a response was waiting for me when I arrived at work the next morning. It was another long one, similar to the e-mail that taught me about the eight elements of change and the four elements of culture. I have provided it in full detail because of the value that it brings to the process of setting and achieving your goals.

To: Todd Bradley
From: TAN

You have made a good start with your steering team. I also like the way you have set up the sub-teams in order to promote some of the eight elements and get further clarity on the items listed. It is now time for you to learn about the Goal Achievement Model, which is the next step in the process. First of all, realize that your list is not a list of only goals. Instead, it is a conglomeration of goals, initiatives, and even some specific activities. As you learn more about the Goal

Achievement Model, you will
learn how to differentiate among
the three types. So let's get
started.

The Eastern Plant has established a vision and communicated
it to the workforce. The three
"P"s for production, performance, and people was a great
idea if you Pat and the others
practice what you preach. If you
do, this concept will make an
impact. But as I am sure you
know, a vision is not enough.
You need to deliver change that
will support the vision and have
the vision be recognized by
everyone, regardless of their
level in the organization. Then
their efforts can directly support the vision you are trying
to establish. The tool that will
enable you and the workforce to
achieve the vision is called the
Goal Achievement Model, or GAM
for short.

The Goal Achievement Model is
composed of seven parts. Let me
show you the model first; then
I'll explain the individual
parts. I'll also give you an
example so that you can see how
the parts function as a collective whole. Although the letters

may not make any sense to you at
this point, they will shortly.

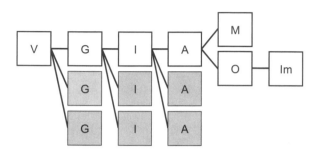

• **V (Vision)** By now you
already have a basic understanding of the concept of a vision
and have developed one for your
plant.

• **G (Goals)** Next you need to
set high-level goals for the
organization that directly support the vision. Goals are
strategic level concepts that
when taken together will enable
you to achieve the vision of
your future. It is also important that you understand that
goals are not specific work
tasks or you will cause yourself
problems in developing the other
parts of the model.

Organizations often list a vast
array of goals because they have
many significant problems to

address right away. Having a
great number of goals is not by
itself a bad thing. However, you
need to recognize that you can
not work on all of them at once.
If you try this approach, you
risk watering down your overall
effort to the point of ineffec-
tiveness. I once worked with
someone who compared this problem to a river that was a mile
wide but only an inch deep.
Trying to complete too many
goals all at once will get you
into trouble and the process
will grind to a halt. If you
identify more goals than you
believe can be addressed at the
same time, prioritize them. Then
work on the first three-to-five.
When one of these is completed,
then and only then add the next
one to your list. Just remember
goals are high-level strategic
concepts. They can not be acted
on directly without a great deal
of additional development.

- **I (Initiatives)** Initiatives
are what many organizations call
programs and are easily recognized. They still have a strategic component, but they are much
more tactical in nature. They
are the specific areas for
improvement identified by the

organization. Just as a vision might have many goals, a goal might have many initiatives. As with goals, you need to be careful how many initiatives the organization tries to address at the same time. If you don't monitor the number, then once again you run the risk of making the total change effort ineffective.

• **A (Activities)** At the activity level, specific work tasks are identified and assigned in order to complete each initiative. Activities are totally tactical. They are extremely specific in nature, focused on completing work assignments to drive the initiative to completion. These are the actual work tasks.

• **M (Measures)** The saying that "what gets measured gets done" is central to this part of the model. All too often managers try to redefine what is meant as measures to something far different than what they were meant to be. The measures important here are not the high-level company performance indicators nor even the measures used to indicate success in achieving the vision, goals, initiatives, or other parts of the process. The measures here specifically track completion of the connected activity. An activity states what is to be done. In turn, the measure clearly defines who is to perform the activity and when they are to complete it.

- **O (Outcomes)** Every activity that you undertake, whether successfully or even unsuccessfully, has one or more outcomes associated with it. These outcomes are the results of what you do. Whether you do it well or poorly, the organization will be affected. The outcome can help promote change, cause change to stagnate, or even worse destroy all or part of what you have accomplished to date.

- **I (Impacts)** Every outcome has an impact on the organization, whether it be on your team, other departments, or even others outside of the company. To complicate matters even more, these impacts may be either positive or negative. To help put these relationships into perspective, let me show you the relationship in the form of a quad diagram - a diagram that

shows how two variables interre-
late.

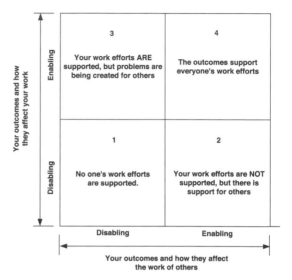

In Block #1, the impacts are
negative for both you and others. You may not believe it, but
at times management drives
activities whose outcomes actually have a negative impact on
everyone. Your analysis of the
outcomes from the activities
should allow you to recognize
when this is about to happen.
This will allow you to address
the impending problem before it
becomes an issue. Negative
impacts across entire organizations can be devastating for any
change initiative.

In Block #2, the impacts are
positive for you, but negative
for others. These others may be
people within your department,
other departments, or even those
with whom you do business. In
any case, negative impacts on
"others" do not help nor support
a collective effort. Therefore,
they are not acceptable as a
result of employing the Goal
Achievement Model.

In Block #3, we have just the
opposite of Block #2 — positive
impacts for others, but negative
ones for you. Avoid any activities that lead you to Block #3.
Otherwise, your effort to make a
change will make anything that
you try to accomplish virtually
impossible because you are negatively impacting yourself. That
is a hurdle which is hard to
overcome.

Block #4 is where you want to
be. In this mode the impacts are
positive for everyone. Imagine
the boost that a change effort
will experience if everyone
involved believes that the
impact from the effort will be
positive for them.

Now for the example that I

promised. Follow it closely so that you will be able to differentiate the various levels of the model. You can then place the items developed by your team on the proper level within the model. This example should also help you fill in the gaps so that your team will have a fully functional model, one that can be used to support the achievement of the vision.

Suppose that your vision is to operate your plant in a way that enables you to run the equipment reliably and meet your customer's demands for product. From this vision, your team creates several goals. Remember that goals provide a high-level strategic direction for the organization that supports the vision. Let's assume you identify three goals.

Vision: Operate your plant in a way that enables you to run the equipment reliably and meet your customer's demands for product.

Goals:
1. Develop a reliability program.
2. Train a reliability-focused workforce.
3. Implement improved spare parts program.

To keep this example simple,
let's just work with one goal
and build on it. The goal I will
select is #1: develop a reliability program. The initiatives
that are associated with this
goal begin the process in which
we will develop the balance of
the model. The goals help us
make the transition from elements that are strategically
focused to those that are tactical in nature. Once again for
our example, the team developed
three initiatives from the goal.

Goal: Develop a reliability
    program
Initiatives:
1. Create a preventive mainte-
    nance (PM) program.
2. Create a predictive mainte-
    nance (PdM) program.
3. Train the workforce in how to
    administer these programs
    efficiently.

As you can see, the items at the
initiative level are like familiar programs from past work
efforts. Creating initiatives is
not by itself the challenge;
initiatives are created all of
the time. The real challenge is
twofold. First, initiatives are

all too often left to stand alone, not tied to goals and certainly not to the vision. This isolation leaves people with initiatives that are not linked to the business and never seem to get done. Frustration will follow and that frustration can easily lead to the failure of any change effort. The second and even greater challenge is that most firms stop at the initiative level or, at best, poorly develop the supporting activities. This failure to complete the model leaves those involved with a semblance of direction, but without any real understanding of how to get where they want to go.

To address this second challenge, we need to develop the activities that support each initiative. These activities will provide the direction that everyone seeks. Let's use the first initiative and list some of the required activities required to accomplish it.

Initiative: Create a preventive
   maintenance (PM) program
Activities:
1. Identify equipment to receive PM.
2. Develop the work scope.
3. Train the workforce.
4. Provide the required tools.
5. Schedule the work.

6.Prepare the equipment and perform the work.
7.Monitor compliance/take corrective action as needed.

The activity list can be long. I
have not listed all of the
activities necessary to make a PM
program functional because I just
wanted you to get the idea.
Also, the list may be long, but
all of the steps do not have to
be accomplished at the same time.
For instance, identifying the
equipment to receive PM and
developing the scope of work are
sequential, not parallel steps.
You can not develop a scope
until you have the equipment
list. Many other activities fall
into this same category, being
sequential rather than parallel.
Nevertheless, you can complete
all of the activities if you
take them on in the proper
order.

Once you have established the
order of the activities, you need
to take the next step, which is
assigning people and due dates to
the various activities. Knowing
the sequence will help you with
your scheduling because the due
dates need to be coordinated with
the sequence of the activities.

For example, using our example, the development of the scope can't start until the equipment list is developed. Knowing this will also help you assign the people who will have the responsibility of performing the work.

Todd, the value of the Goal Achievement Model is that all of the parts fit together into a seamless process. Therefore, people working on what they may consider a mundane task can clearly see how their efforts support the initiatives, which in turn support the goals and ultimately the vision. I can show this to you using the simple example that I just provided.

Vision: Operate your plant in a way that enables you to run the equipment reliably and meet your customer's demands for product.
Goal: Develop a reliability program.
Initiative: Create a preventive maintenance (PM) program.
Activity: Identify equipment to receive PM.

In this example, the mechanics who identify the equipment

that will be included in the PM program can see how their work supports the vision of the plant. The model is powerful because everyone is aligned to a common purpose. The model provides another side benefit. If for some reason you are working on an activity that can not be linked through the Goal Achievement Model back to the vision, you are likely to be working on the wrong thing.

So, now you know about the Goal Achievement Model. It isn't very hard to build, but it is important to get the items in their correct place. Don't forget to review the outcomes and impacts from the work done within the model. Remember there are always outcomes. However, you want them to be positive for all to assure your success.

Good luck
TAN

Once again TAN had provided me with the strategy we would need to create our vision and develop accompanying goals, initiatives, and activities. If the steering team could develop its own complete Goal Achievement Model, and then distribute both the concept and the actual work out to the plant, I felt certain we would succeed. The question in my mind was not what to do, but how to do it. Then I remembered the list we had created at our steering team meeting.

What if I could fit these items into a goal achievement model of our own? Then, after explaining this new approach to the team, we could fill in the missing parts. In essence we would have developed our own model. If we all understood the concept and were able to build the full model, then surely we would figure out how to enact it. I remembered then that we had to develop measures for the activities so that we could track our progress as well, and also evaluate the outcome and impacts so we could assure success for all.

In my mind, there are essentially two ways for a team to develop the changes that need to be implemented, in our case the Goal Achievement Model. The first is to start with a blank sheet of paper and build the entire model from scratch. The second way is to begin with what is often called a "strawman.' Rather than beginning with a blank sheet, a strawman provides a preliminary framework to get the group started; it often focuses them as well.

The blank sheet approach takes considerably more time than the strawman approach, which I thought would work better for our team because 1) we didn't have a lot of time (the site visit was fast approaching) and 2) we had already completed some of the preliminary work. We had already made our list of what at the time we thought were our goals. I chose to use the strawman approach, hoping to help move the process along faster. However, I did not want to appear dictatorial in my approach.

After digesting TAN's comments about the Goal Achievement Model, I recognized clearly that the list we had developed was not all goals. Building a strawman while fitting the list to the model was going to require some work. We had already established the vision, so that level of the model was already completed. The next was the section for goals. TAN had told me that these were high-level strategic concepts, not mere tactical plans that were able to be addressed by immediate action. TAN's example helped me see the difference.

The list we had developed included goals, initiatives, and even some activities. Sorting the items was not going to be an easy task. After a few hours, I was not getting anywhere and instead was beginning to get depressed and frustrated. I thought that taking a break might help. So I walked through the plant, checking on the maintenance work that was taking place and talking with some of the workers. Such walks not only help me do my job, but they keep me connected to how the plant is really operating. Today I hoped that my walk would provide insight into how people were reacting to the communications meeting. I also hoped the walk would help me refocus on our goals within the context of the Goal Achievement Model. After all, I had to have the strawman ready for our meeting the following morning.

One hour later I had finished my tour and was heading back to the office. The plant was running as well as could be expected, and I had heard some very positive feedback from many of the workers. Although most were still skeptical, they liked what Pat and I had said; they were beginning to entertain some hope for our future. However, I had not even begun to figure out how I was going to take the list we had developed and turn it into a strawman Goal Achievement Model

As I was leaving the production area, I almost collided with Gene Smith, the union president and newly appointed member of the steering team. We talked briefly about the communication meeting and the work he was doing with Sally to clarify the goals. In fact, he was headed to her office when we met. As we concluded our conversation, he smiled and raised his left hand palm outward with three fingers extended; his thumb holding down his pinky finger

I was confused. "Gene, what are you doing?"

Still smiling he said as he touched each of his three fingers with his right hand, "production, performance, and people."

I smiled also expecting this to be some sort of joke. "Where did you make that up?"

"I didn't," he said.

"So who did"?"

"I don't know."

"So who is using this new sign of the times," I asked, still assuming that he was just teasing me.

"Everyone," he said as he turned and left to find Sally.

I was thrilled. This new sign of the times indicated that the desire for change to something better was taking hold. At the same time, I knew we needed to do more to make a real impact. When I reached my office, I was ready to get back to work. If goals were high-level strategic concepts in support of the vision, then what better goals were there than the ones we had already inadvertently developed: production, performance, and people? Of course, they needed to be embellished. Still, it was clear to me that I had discovered the three goals that I was going to use for the Goal Achievement Model. My next step was to link initiatives to the goals. As TAN had informed me, initiatives were the undertakings that an organization would commonly call programs. The difference is that programs often fail because they are developed without linkages to goals and the vision. Initiatives, by virtue of being part of an entire goal model, had a much greater likelihood of success. Looking at our list, I now linked the items that were clearly initiatives to the three goals. When I was finished, my first pass at our Goal Achievement Model looked like this:

Vision: We will operate our plant so that equipment never fails in an unplanned fashion. This high level of reliability will enable us to continually supply the demands of our customers as well as take on new ones. We will perform this work in a way that recognizes the important and unique value that each person brings to the effort.

Goals	Initiatives
Production – Operate the equipment properly to consistently meet customer's demands.	1. Obtain the Epsilon contract. 2. Convert Line #1 to Epsilon production. 3. Develop Line #2 to run all products including Epsilon. 4. Operate Lines #3 and #4 in a flexible manner for all products excluding Epsilon.
Performance – Maintain and operate the equipment in a reliable manner at all times.	1. Institute a PM program. 2. Institute a PdM program. 3. Implement a reliability-focused repair process. 4. Conduct failure analysis and corrective action for all line shutdowns.
People – Treat all people as critical parts of the team with dignity and respect.	1. Employ teams at the lines and throughout the plant. 2. Communicate via forums and other means.

Initially I was going to limit the number of initiatives, but decided against it. I recognized that I could list more initiatives than we were capable of handling. Yet if that turned out to be the case, we could always prioritize them and work the lower priority items at a later date. I did not want to run the risk of not listing something that the team would have considered important.

Although I had my own ideas for additional initiatives, I decided to focus on the list the team developed so that it wouldn't appear that I was trying to direct the process. As part of the team's training, I wanted them to be able to add items. In this way, they would learn about the Goal Achievement Model and share ownership of the final product. Meanwhile, I could still use the strawman approach to speed up our effort.

After a great deal of work with the model, I was finished. I had started with our vision and the list we had created at our meeting. Now I had our goals (the three Ps) and a first pass at the initiatives. Clarifying the initiatives as well as identifying activities, measures, outcomes, and impacts was the steering team's responsibility as they learned first hand about the goal model. I was grateful both to TAN for showing me this very useful model and to the steering team for the list we had developed. I made my copies of the model in progress and was ready for the scheduled steering team meeting.

CHAPTER 8

LINE #3 GOES DOWN AGAIN

Sometimes your best laid plans don't always work out. Even though the next day dawned sunny and bright, and I was prepared for our steering team meeting, the plant equipment had other plans for us. I should have known that we were in store for a major problem. The lines had been running well, all too well, and the morale of the employees appeared to be starting to change.

When I got to work, I grabbed my hard hat and my radio and did what I have done every day during my tenure at the Eastern Plant. I went out to visit the four tractium lines to make sure they were running as planned. In fact, everything was just fine. My rounds completed, I returned to the office to assemble the handouts for the steering team meeting. I also wanted to prepare myself mentally so that I could help the team understand and apply the Goal Achievement Model. Just as I was ready to head over to the conference room, I got a call on the radio. With the removal of the hideous Line Down alarm several days ago, radio communication was now the established method to alert the management team that we were having a serious problem somewhere in the plant. The call was coming in from one of the operators on Line #3.

"This is Ben on Line #3. We have had a major shutdown of the line and we need everyone to respond. We are in the process of securing the equipment. Please respond."

"Ben, Todd here. I will be right over," I said as I left the office, not for the steering team meeting but to find out what had happened on Line #3. When I arrived, I saw Pat, Gene, and several steering team members who had been assigned radios at the plant communication meeting. They had all responded. They were standing at the base of the line looking at the shredded main belt — the same belt that had shredded on my first day and, of course, many times afterwards.

In the old culture, Mike and the maintenance team would have already been tearing the equipment apart so that maintenance could make the repair and get the line back in service. Not this time. We had promised the employees that things were going to be different. We had promised them that we were not going to make rapid repairs to get the equipment back on line until we knew why the equipment had failed in the first place. Now was the time to put our actions in place in support of what we had told everyone. I could see that Pat was ready to jump right in and start tearing out the failed belt in the style of Mike Kane. However, Gene grabbed his arm and whispered something in his ear. Pat calmed down and walked over to speak with the operators. I leaned over to Gene and asked, "What did you tell Pat? For a moment there it looked like he was going to start acting like Mike."

Gene smiled and raised his hand palm outward with three fingers extended and said, "I just reminded him about the three Ps, specifically the one about performance, in this case reliability performance. I also reminded him that he and the rest of us needed to practice what we preached the other day or the whole effort would go down the drain."

I thanked him and then using my loudest voice I attempted to get everyone's attention. It wasn't easy with all of the people in the immediate area, but after a moment everyone stopped talking and gave me their attention. Unbeknownst to those present, we were about to engage in root cause failure analysis. We would find out once and for all why Line #3 and sometimes Line #4 were shutting down with belt failures. This work wasn't something I needed TAN to explain. I knew what to do from having used root cause failure analysis at my former job. It was a shame for ATPCo that Doug never let me figure out why he had so many reliability problems. As far as even suggesting it to Mike; well I was smarter than that.

Looking around I saw that the operators were in the final stages of shutting down the line and making it safe for work. I instructed the production foreman not to disturb any of the evidence while they were making the line safe. They were also to mark down all dial and switch settings so that we would know the readings and positions at the time of failure. Fortunately I had my radio and had arrived at the scene early. As a result, I was able to pass on this directive before much of the evidence was disturbed. I also told the foreman that we would speak with each operator to find out from them first-hand what had happened.

With Gene present for union support, I told the foreman that he could tell everyone on the crew, and anyone else he cared to tell, that we vitally needed their information. There would be no punishment whatsoever for anything that we found, even items that could be attributed to operator error. Both the foreman and Gene were surprised by this statement, but I knew that we had a much better chance of getting to the truth if no one felt threatened.

As I surveyed the area, I noticed that all of the members of the steering team were there. Pat, his department heads Pete and Sally, and Gene had responded because they had been issued radios at our communications meeting and told to respond in this type of emergency. Nick and Dani had been on their way to the steering team meeting. When they saw the other team members heading for Line #3, they simply followed along. Therefore, I had seven people there, including myself, readily available and possessing a great deal of diverse background to help with our effort. I gathered them all together and described what we were going to do.

"Team," I said. "We are about to embark on an effort called Root Cause Failure Analysis or RCFA for short. This process is going to help us find out why the belt on Line #3 failed. Our goal is to fix the problem so that it never happens again. To do this, I am going to divide you up into three teams, each with a different responsibility to gather evidence about this failure. You may think that this will be something that you can do in the next hour or two. But as you begin to understand what it is you have to do, you will quickly think otherwise. We want to do this right. However, we also have other pressing problems. Therefore, I am going to give the sub-teams two days to accomplish their work.

" Sally and Gene, I want you to gather the people evidence. Talk with the operators who were working at the time of the failure. Talk with every other operator on Line #3 because most likely at some point in their career they were working when one of these belts failed. We need to know everything that they know or even think that they know. Gene, people trust you as their union president. You can relate to them what I told you and the line foreman just a few minutes ago. There will be no punishment. Call it amnesty if you like for everyone, no matter what information is revealed or what facts are discovered. In this way we can be sure that all of the people-related facts will be uncovered."

I knew Gene was the right person for this task because of his high standing with the hourly workers. After all, he had been elected to three consecutive two-year terms as union president. Sally was also the right person to team with Gene. She had an extensive engineering background and could analyze what was learned in a very objective light. Together they would give the team a well-rounded view of what the people involved thought and saw.

I could tell that Pat didn't like the amnesty idea, but I knew I was on solid ground. Normally I would have put a caveat on my statement so that if willful negligence was uncovered, the amnesty would be revoked. However we had experienced so many failures that it would have been virtually impossible for one individual to cause all of them. In addition, we had a lot more failures in the plant besides the belt. We needed everyone to help us figure out why things failed. It also was one of the three Ps — in this case people —and we had to start trusting people and working as a team. Now was as good a time as any. As a last thought, I also told Gene and Pat to talk with the maintenance mechanics — anyone who had ever worked on the line as well as anyone else who had even the most remote involvement with the line. That applied to all departments.

Next I turned to Pete (the new Production Manager) and Dani. "I want the two of you to address what I will call 'position' and 'parts.' Within position, there are two areas to explore. First find out what the settings were on the dials and the readings on the gages. This information should be available because I told the foreman to have the operators record all of this information as they were shutting the line down. Second, find out where everyone was when the failure occurred as well as what they were doing. You will need to get this information from the operators, but don't interview them. Just get the positional information; we will analyze it all later.

I also want you to gather up any and all information you can find about the parts. This includes the obvious: the failed belt itself. But also gather information about the other parts we use on this machine. Who knows? There may be something in all of the parts-related information that will help us solve this problem." I had picked Pete and Dani for obvious reasons. They both knew the machine from the inside out based on their operating experience. If there was any evidence regarding either position or parts that would help our analysis, they would dig it out.

Last but not least, I assigned Pat and Nick the task of gathering and reviewing all of the related paper — the documentation related to the line. This documentation included everything from the technical manuals for the equipment to the work order when the belt was last installed. For a plant that had been in existence as long as the Eastern Plant, this task was not a small one. Yet somewhere in all of that paper might be the answer we sought.

It was still early in the day. Everyone had plenty of time to begin their assignments, which were scheduled to conclude two days hence. The plan was that we would gather in the conference room in two days with all of the information we had gathered and begin the analysis.

Now you may be thinking that we had abandoned our long-term effort for a short term crisis, getting the line running, but I would strongly disagree. Our new vision was founded on the three Ps. Performance was one of them. We had talked about performance at the communication meeting; I had told everyone things were going to be different. If we were going to succeed with our longer-term vision, we needed to put our words into action. Everyone was watching. If we faltered for even one second, we were lost. As everyone was leaving to work on their tasks, I wished them luck. I raised my left hand palm outward with three fingers raised and smiled. The last thing I saw before I turned away was Gene's wink and smile.

Two days later when the team assembled in the conference room, even I was amazed at the amount of information that had been acquired. Sally and Gene had interview documentation from every operator: those on duty at the time of the failure and everyone else. No one had refused the interview after Gene had explained the amnesty rule. To the surprise of everyone on our team, people actually came into work on their own time to be interviewed and share their knowledge. They also had interview sheets from the mechanics who had worked on the line and the warehouse. They also spoke with one engineer, Scott Schaeffer, who had previously tried to solve this problem until Mike had threatened him with the highway and made him stop.

Pete and Dani had gone over the machine from top to bottom. They had all of the gage and dial settings at the time of failure. They had also documented where everyone had been standing and what they had been doing. Once again, the documentation was extensive. They had even found the time to compare the settings at the time of failure with the design and operation manual. They also had photographed the belt and carefully looked it over for any apparent flaws. The failed piece had been sent to a lab for more detailed analysis and the information was due later in the day. Finally, they had listings of all the parts that had been ordered and when. This information covered parts that had not failed, those that were on the shelf in the warehouse, and those we

didn't stock but were available from the equipment manufacturer.

As for Pat and Nick, they had gathered boxes of
paper related to the equipment. In fact, they had so many
boxes that they needed help to bring them all to the conference room. To my surprise they had even had time to
index everything so that they could pull it quickly from
the file boxes as we needed it.

After congratulating them for all of their hard
work I got right down to business. "You may be wonder-
ing what we are going to do with all this information. We
are going to use it to determine exactly why the line belt
failed. Once we know the reason, we are going to correct
it for all time. This process will not only solve our immediate problem, but it will also reinforce the performance
part of the three Ps with the organization. So let's get
started.

"The first thing we want to do is clearly define the
problem we are trying to solve. Before any of you say
anything, think about how we want to define our problem so that we state it specifically. If we aren't exact, we
have the chance of getting off track and not really getting to the root." After quite a bit of discussion, we determined that our statement of the problem was that the
Line #3 belt catastrophically failed, causing the line to
shut down with the resultant loss of production. Once
we agreed, I wrote our problem statement on the flip
chart I had brought to the room for this purpose.

My next challenge to the team was to ask why this
problem occurred. We brainstormed all of the reasons
why we thought that this was possible. To my surprise
after a great deal of discussion, the team arrived at seven
possibilities. The following diagram reproduces the flip

chart to this point.

I explained to the team that the next step was to ask ourselves why we thought that each of the selected reasons for the line failure happened. As a ground rule, we were not to be judgmental or analyze the identified reason why, but instead just list it. After we had made our list, we would go back and discuss each reason. We would use our evidence to determine the likelihood that the reason for failure we were addressing could actually be the reason. We would score each item either 1 (unlikely), 3 (possible), or 5 (highly likely). We would then repeat the process for the elements that scored a 5.

The goal was to drill down through the items, building what is referred to as a "Why Tree." Eventually we would get to the root causes of the problem, often an inappropriate action by a human being, which in turn set the process of eventual failure in place. I could tell that my last statement got their attention, especially Pat who had been somewhat critical of my amnesty rule related to the line belt failure. I needed to clarify my last statement. Otherwise, I thought that Pat and maybe some others would be looking for someone to blame (and pun-

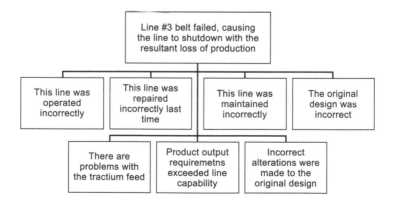

The Problem Statement

Line #3 belt failed numerous times over the last two years, causing the line to shut down with the resultant loss of production

Why – Level 1	Why – Level 2	Score	Score Reason/ Evidence
The line was operated incorrectly.	The operators were not properly trained.	1	Operators had been working the line for years and were experienced.
	There were new products being run and the wrong method was used.	1	The line was running the same products it had run since it was built.
	Operators made adjustments that were incorrect.	1	The evidence stated that no adjustments were made that were incorrect.
The line was repaired incorrectly.	Mechanics were not properly trained.	1	Some new mechanics worked on the belt but they were part of teams with more experienced employees.
	Wrong tools were used.	1	The same tools had been used since the machine was built. No changes in the last two years.
	Wrong parts were used.	3	The parts were taken out of the warehouse, but an examination of the records showed that at times there were stocking errors.
	The wrong repair procedure was employed.	1	The same procedure was used since the line was built. It was the one in the manual.
The line was maintained incorrectly.	No preventive maintenance (FM)	5	PM was not part of the maintenance work effort.
	No predictive maintenance (PdM)	5	PdM was not part of the maintenance work effort.
	No operator minor maintenance	3	Operator minor maintenance was not part of the maintenance work effort.
The original design was incorrect.	Bad design specification	1	This was believed to be less significant than PM and PdM.
The tractium feed was of wrong or of poor quality.	Wrong feed brought into the line	1	The lines were all the same and #1 and #2 had no problems. All feeds are the same to the lines.
	Poor quality feed brought into the line	1	If this were the case, all lines would have problems and this is not the case.
The line capacity was exceeded.	Customer demands and poor reliability resulted in running beyond capacity to catch up.	3	Production records and interviews clearly indicate that the lines were at time run beyond capacity to meet demand.
Alterations were made to the equipment	No procedure is in place to assure that the correct changes were being made.	5	A review of all of the paper along with interviews supported that no procedure was ever developed.

ish).

"I need to get something clear in everyone's mind before we begin," I said. "This process isn't about finding a scapegoat to blame and punish. It isn't about people themselves. Instead, the process is about the decision-making processes that we use which in turn set the stage for failure.

"Let's use an example that we can all relate to: preventive maintenance (PM). Assume that 1) we had a line failure and 2) we identified that the root cause was that the line mechanics didn't conduct the preventive maintenance when it was planned. Why? Because they had been diverted to several emergency jobs and were never able to get back to the PM tasks. As a result, the line failed. Do we punish the mechanics?"

I left this question hanging in the air, waiting for someone the answer it. After a moment, Pete said, "No, we can't punish the mechanics. Although they didn't perform the PM, it was management that forced them to stop the PM and move on to the emergency work."

I thanked Pete and said, "That's it exactly. We don't punish the mechanics. We punish, or more accurately, we change the management system that enabled the inappropriate human action. One last thing: we work on our Why Tree until we identify and correct the root causes. In doing so, we can correct our problem."

With that we began discussing the first two levels of the Why Tree. It took a long time, but in the end we had identified a lot of possibilities and had ranked the Level Two reasons with our 1-3-5 scale. Our work is shown in tabular form so that you can see the results. I have also listed the reasons and evidence that supported the scores so that you can understand the reasoning for each item's score.

Examining the Why Tree through two levels was revealing to the team. Because of all of the evidence they had collected, they were able to eliminate many of the suspected reasons why the belt failed. What we decided to do was to work first on the "whys" that scored 5. We would see if we could go another level deeper into the Why Tree. While the team was at lunch, I reworked the flip chart, focusing on those listings that scored a 5. This new chart, vastly reduced in size, helped the team to focus.

When everyone returned from lunch, I told them

Why – Level 1	Why – Level 2	Score	Score Reason/ Evidence
The line was maintained incorrectly.	No preventive maintenance (PM)	5	PM was not part of the maintenance work effort.
	No predictive maintenance (PdM)	5	PdM was not part of the maintenance work effort.
Alterations were made to the equipment without validation.	No procedure is in place to assure that the correct changes were being made.	5	A review of all of the paper along with interviews supported that no procedure was ever developed.

that we were going to drill down one more layer so that we could ultimately fix the problem. The first question I asked was, "Why was there no preventive maintenance program?" The answers suggested by the team were:

- PM was not considered important. The focus was on production and rapid repair.
- There was no PM planned into the process.
- Plant emergencies took up everyone's time so there was no time for PM.
- Management did not support a PM program.

- The operators would not have shut down anyway even if a PM program had been in place.

"Let's distill these answers down to one, if possible, because I think we are on to something," I said.

Sally spoke up before the others and commented, "All of these answers are really one and the same. A management decision was made not to support or put into place a preventive maintenance program for the tractium lines. In other words, folks," she said addressing the team. "We have a root cause for the failure."

"Not so quick," I responded. "Let's look at this Why Tree and see if it explains the belt failure, which is the issue that we are examining. Let's do it by working our way down the tree. The line belt failed. Why? Because the line was maintained incorrectly. Why? Because no PM program was in place. Why? Because management didn't support this type of work. With this logic in place, if we had a PM program, would we have prevented the belt from continuously failing?"

Sally looked crestfallen. She admitted that the answer most likely was no. All that a PM program would have done is to have the maintenance mechanics change the belt more frequently. It would still fail, but we would replace it before it failed catastrophically, shutting down the line. With some discussion, the group admitted that this was true not only for a PM program, but also for a predictive maintenance program (PdM).

With that, we turned our attention to the why that addressed incorrect alterations to the line. To kick off this discussion, I asked, "Were there ever any modifications made to the line?" If the answer was no, then we were once again headed down the wrong path. But that wasn't the answer that Pat and Nick provided. Yes, there had been numerous modifications over the years, even before Mike had arrived on the scene.

The next question then was, "Why was no procedure in place to assure that correct changes were being made?" Once again, the evidence revealed the answer. The changes were all designed and made by the equipment manufacturer after extensive testing witnessed by the customers, ATPCo being one of them. That made sense to me. We still had a problem, however, in that we had no internal procedure to review and validate the change before we made it to our equipment.

"Let me ask you one more question about changes to the line," I said. "I realize that the equipment manufacturer developed and made all of the changes. But did that apply to every one of the changes, even the very minor changes that an equipment vendor would not normally handle?"

The answer came from Nick, who was waving some paperwork which he had just pulled from his files. "Todd, the answer is no. We have made simple changes and minor additions in which the vendor was not involved. I have three right here. I can pull more from these files if you would like."

"And these did not follow a change management process?" I asked.

"No," Nick said, "Because as we have seen from the investigation, no change management process existed."

We pulled out all of the various pieces of paper documenting the minor changes and reviewed them in great detail. By now it was getting late and everyone was tired. I was almost ready to call it a day when Sally, who was reviewing one of the memos about a change, cried out, "Oh my God!" That caught everyone's attention. The tiredness we were all feeling left the room.

"Here is one of the minor changes, but I think it is going to amaze all of you," she said. "Just slightly over two years ago, right before we started experiencing the belt failures, Mike put out the memo that I have right here. In it, he stated that he wanted all of the Bills of Material for the lines to reflect all of the parts that we stocked in the warehouse for that line. We had listed the belts for Lines #1 and #2 in their Bills of Material, but had never put the part numbers into the material lists for Lines #3 and #4. So we added the belts.

"Because we were short of ATPCo resources, we used summer interns. Not having a process to validate all the changes is where we missed the boat because the belt part number was 31X21793GL and the intern entered 31X21739GL in the material lists for Lines #3 and #4. Folks, the belt failure problem we have been having is because the intern transposed two numbers. With the wrong part number on the material list, we have been ordering and installing the wrong belt."

When I looked around the room I could see that everyone was in a state of shock. A simple error of two transposed numbers had caused all of the belt problems for the last two years. Not wanting to lose the moment, I said, "Let's put this information into our Why Tree and see the results." I wrote it on the flip chart and have reproduced it for your information. This diagram clearly showed everyone why the belts had failed over the last two years. It also showed how to correct the problem so that at least this error would never happen again.

Although the immediate answer was to fix the bill of material and get the right belt installed, the solution had far broader impact. We were going to write and implement a procedure that would prevent equipment alterations of any sort without first having a multi-functional review. I also pointed out that the root cause appeared to be a mistake made by an individual, but was really a flaw in our management system. Punishing the individual would serve no purpose in this case or any other of this nature.

At this point, I was not just tired. I was exhausted and could tell that the others felt the same way. I knew

Line #3 belt failed, causing the line to shut down with the resultant loss of production

Why?

Alterations were made to the equipment without validation

Why?

No procedure was in place to assure that correct changes are being made

Why?

It wasn't needed - the changes were made by the vendor and checked before installation

But

Minor changes that did not originate with the vendor were also made and were not checked

And the result was...

When the belts were added to the bill of material for Line #3 & #4, a code error was made and the wrong belt purchased

that by the next morning everyone in the plant would know what we had accomplished. We had not just solved the belt problem, but had also lived up to our promise to stress performance and make long-lasting reliability-based repairs. I didn't know it at the time, but what the team had learned about root cause failure analysis would come into play later on as we worked to implement our longer-term improvement strategy.

CHAPTER 9

A New Role Model is in Town

We needed all of the time available to us to get the plant ready for the visit by our future customer. Already we had lost several days of preparation as we worked our way through the root cause failure analysis for Line #3, but it had been worth it. We had taken a major step towards permanently improving our plant's reliability. We had visibly demonstrated our commitment to the vision. Furthermore, as a team we had learned some skills that would help us work together in a far more efficient manner. Nevertheless, we had lost two days plus the weekend, and the customer review was only 76 days away — 55 days if you didn't count the weekends. We desperately needed to get re-focused on the task at hand — improving our overall reliability.

At 9:00 AM, the steering team reconvened. We were very happy about the results of the RCFA on Line #3 because we had found the root cause of a long standing problem. Most of the team could not believe how such a simple error could have caused such a long-term problem. I could tell from the conversation that they were not only happy about the outcome, but also they recognized the root issues associated with it. We could fix the specific problem of the wrong belt being used. At the same time, we could take steps to see that similar problems were avoided in the future.

After a while, however, it was now time to get back to the work at hand. "What do the numbers 76 and 55 mean to all of you?" I asked. No one seemed to know the answer because all I got from the team was a collective blank stare. I let them think about it for a moment and then answered my own question. "Those numbers are how long we have until our prospective customer's visit: 76 calendar days and 55 workdays. Folks, we don't have a lot of time to get the whole plant functioning in a reliable fashion." That got their attention because everyone clearly recognized that our time was indeed short.

In addition to actually getting the team working again, Pat and I had a second problem. Allen was getting restless. Last week, our first status meeting had not been well received. Allen was looking for a definitive set of work steps that, when completed, would provide the reliable plant operation he expected. We didn't have one then and we still didn't have one. In fact, we were not even going to be building one in the shape and form Allen expected. We were headed in a different direction. We were going to develop the Goal Achievement Model and achieve what I expected to be better and longer lasting than a simple timeline with related tasks.

Of course we could create what Allen wanted — an activity chart with due dates — but as I had learned from TAN, that was the start down the road to ultimate failure. Tasks or activities without linkages to initiatives, goals, and ultimately the Eastern Plant's vision were just a waste of time, a commodity that we didn't have. The problem was that Allen didn't know this. What he expected was not aligned with what we were doing.

The immediate task that Pat and I faced was to keep Allen satisfied while we followed a process that would deliver long-term sustainable value well beyond acquiring the tractium contract. Our conference call with Allen was scheduled for the next day so we had until then to figure out what we were going to tell him. I hoped that the work we were about to do within the steering team, along with our success on Lines #3 and #4, would give us enough information so that we could continue to move forward and satisfy Allen as well, but I wasn't sure.

The team wanted to begin where we left off at our first meeting. Many had ideas about the meaning of many of the listed items. After all, that was the task that I had assigned the sub-teams as we ended our last meeting. They had all done their homework. In order to gather their ideas, recognize their efforts, and (unknown to them) position the team to learn about and apply the Goal Achievement Model, we spent time discussing each item on the list. This process took a long time because there were many diverse opinions about the meaning behind many of the items.

I have re-created the list (on the next page), along with the meaning that the team finally assigned to each. Not shown is all of the work that it took to reach consensus.

At this juncture, the group was satisfied with the work that they had accomplished but also frustrated because they didn't think they had made much progress to solve the problems of the plant. After all, where was the work plan that took our list and provided direction to increase plant reliability?

At this point, I explained the goal achievement model, Using TAN's example and one I created, I showed how the pieces fit together. Getting the team to fully understand the model took a considerable amount of time. If we were to succeed, however, having the team understand this concept was extremely important.

Next we turned to the list we had created. I could tell from the conversation that the team realized that many of these items were not goals. "So if what we have are not goals, what goals we are going to use to support the vision?" Pete asked.

"I had an idea when I was preparing for this meeting yesterday," I said. "It is something we created without even realizing we were establishing our goal list. How about the three Ps? They are the strategic direction we have agreed upon. As such, they fit the definition of

Items on the List	Team Assigned Meaning
Become more reliable.	Eliminate the existing quick fix work process. Make equipment more reliable so that it doesn't fail. Utilize RCFA techniques.
Treat people with dignity and respect.	People are the most important part of the business.People make the business a success or a failure. A whole person needs to be engaged in the work effort, not just from the neck down.
Convert Line #1 to Epsilon	Self-explanatory if we want to be awarded the contract.
Understand why equipment fails and correct it forever.	Part of becoming more reliable. We now know a good technique for this based on our RCFA experience with Line #3.
Win the Epsilon contract; pass the review.	Self-explanatory. Required if our business is to be successful.
Stay in business.	This is a component of our vision.
No unplanned line shutdowns..	Part of becoming a more reliable plant
Develop a PM / PdM maintenance program.	Part of becoming a more reliable plant.
Improve our repair process.	The team elected to drop this item because it seems to be closely tied to rapid repair.
Institute the three Ps.	Agreed that these should be our guiding principles for the change process being instituted at the plant.
Better treatment of operators	This was dropped because the team considered it to be an integral part with the items describing the treatment of people with dignity and respect.
Change to a better way of working and make it stick.	The team decided to drop this item as well. They thought that this was an overriding purpose and adequately covered in the vision.
Eliminate the rapid repair process.	Dropped because the team considered that it was addressed in the other items on the list such as becoming a more reliable operation.

| Include reliability engineers in the repair proocess. | As a part of the effort to become more reliable recognize the value that reliability engineers can contribute. Include them as an integral part of the work process. |

the goals within the goal achievement model. What do you think of that as our approach?"

With only a brief discussion, everyone agreed (as I expected they would). Their support came not because we had created three Ps as part of our change effort, but because everyone really believed that the three Ps were exactly what we were trying to accomplish. Additionally everyone could clearly see how these goals directly supported our vision and they were beginning to understand the goal achievement model.

Our next step involved creating initiatives and activities. For that we turned to our list. Reviewing each of the items and with some discussion, we were able to identify which items we thought were initiatives and which were activities. We also added additional activities to our list. They were necessary if we ever hoped to achieve the initiatives, goals, and ultimately our vision.

As it turns out, the goal achievement model I created in my office looked remarkably similar to what the team created. Some would say this similarity came about because I manipulated the group —having already created a goal achievement model, I knew what I wanted the team's model to look like and directed the team accordingly. I disagree. I believe that doing the work in advance of the team meeting enabled me to better facilitate the work process and deliver a much more valuable outcome. If I had wanted to manipulate the team I would've handed out the strawman, skipped the development of the goals and initiatives, and moved straight to the activities, assuming that what I had developed was what we were going to use. This would have been a really bad idea. The group needed to understand the whole model if they were going to be able to teach it to others and support its use.

We were not done. However, we were tired, having spent virtually the entire day to get to this point. We agreed to resume the next day to continue working on the activities, outcomes, and impacts. We also agreed to transfer the flip charts to text format and make copies of what we had developed to that point. Thus, we could use this information as a starting point at our next meeting. The team agreed that if I wanted to I would do some word-smithing to make the document easier to read.

Although it was late, Pat and I still needed to figure out what we were going to tell Allen. We adjourned to Pat's office to discuss the upcoming conference call. We both remembered the last call. It was long and unpleasant. Mike hadn't been gone that long, and Pat and I were working hard not only to take control but also to set a new reliability-focused direction. Allen didn't seem to care as much about our long-term efforts; he was concerned that we produce a detailed work plan to win the Epsilon contract. It eluded me how he could fail to see that they were linked events. After all, if we won the contract but could not run a reliable plant we were lost. Of course we would have the contract at least initially, but our unreliable operation would soon become apparent. The contract would evaporate as if it had never existed.

Pat and I needed to give Allen what he wanted. At the same time, we could not let his approach cause us to deviate from what we both truly believed was the right and longer course of action. "Todd, do you know what Allen wants?" Pat said as he closed his door. "I know how to operate the lines but I have to admit I have never built a work plan of the type Allen expects us to develop.

"Sure, I know exactly what he wants. He wants a chart with time on the x-axis and the sequential steps we're going to take listed on the y-axis. Then with this information, we draw horizontal lines for each task showing how they are linked and how long they will take. It is basically a project work plan with the job steps laid out over a set time period, which in our case is from now until the visit."

"But won't that be difficult to develop considering we are looking at a much longer time frame and a far different approach to the work?" Pat asked. "After all, we are just beginning to identify our initiatives. Not only that, but remember how angry Allen got last time when you started talking about longer-term reliability goals? Those goals sure didn't appear to be anything Allen was interested in. All he wanted was the Epsilon contract. He had no desire to hear about any longer-term plans."

"That's just the point, Pat. Allen is applying reactive business thinking to the problem. It is the same way Mike, or my former boss Doug, thought about problems. All they considered was fixing the problem staring them in the face. They fixed it as quickly as they could so they could get the line running, but they didn't fix the root of the problem. With Lines #3 and #4, it was the wrong belt. With maintenance in general, it was the wrong approach. Now with the Epsilon contract, it is the short-term solution to a long-term problem.

"We need to give Allen what he believes he needs: the short-term work plan. But we need to do so in a way that we not only get the contract but we keep it. And maybe along the way we even pick up a few more contracts. In other words, my friend, we need to help Allen accomplish his goal as well as the one he hasn't even recognized yet."

"So how we do that?" Pat asked.

"It's simpler than you realize, Pat. What we do is create Allen's timeline in the context of the goal achievement model so that we show him what we are doing. Then we tie it into how we are going to get the tractium contract. We need to provide enough detail to satisfy him without sidetracking our process."

I was not sure Pat was convinced, but I took his nod for least tacit approval. So working together for the rest of the afternoon and into the evening, we created the following timeline.

We added written detail that we could explain to Allen at the teleconference. We also made sure we focused on Allen's perceived outcome of success: the

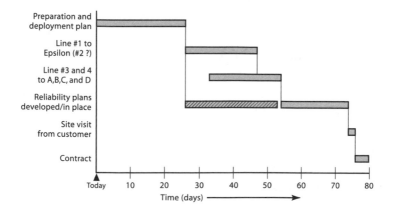

tractium contract. On the surface, it looked exactly like the type of chart that Allen would want. It showed in reasonable detail the steps we were planning to take to win the contract. In short, it addressed what I thought was Allen's reactive mindset. Considering that Allen thought in this manner as leader of ATPCo, it made sense to me how people like Doug McDonald and Mike Kane could achieve leadership positions and promulgate reactive thinking throughout the company. It all went back to what TAN had told me about culture and specifically the element of role models.

In this case, Allen was the central role model. By emulating his behavior, Doug and Mike succeeded. In turn, they were emulated by others at their respective sites — at least by those who were not fired. In the end, emulating reactive leaders allowed reactive thinking to permeate the entire organization. I also realized how difficult changing the culture was going to be in both the short and long term.

The next day began with a great deal of rain, thunder, lightning, and even some local flooding. As I drove to work, I hoped this weather was not a forecast of the rest of my day. Our team meeting was scheduled for eight o'clock, and Pat and I also needed time to prepare for a 3:00 teleconference with Allen. I had taken home for review the work I had done prior to yesterday's meeting. When I compared it with our flip charts and our notes made during the evening, I noted that everything we had discussed fit within the goal achevement model I had developed. Rather than change the wording, I decided to make copies of my list. If the team then wanted to change any wording after our review, I would make the corrections. After some discussion, they didn't really see a need to change anything. Within the first hour of the meeting, we had reached consensus.

The next step was going to be slightly more difficult: the creation of activities. We had ten initiatives. My fear was that if we created four-to-six activities for each initiative, we would have an unmanageable list. However, in his last e-mail TAN explained how to resolve this issue, by prioritizing the list.

Everyone must have reached the same conclusion about what to do next. As the meeting began, the group all spoke at once describing the activities they thought should be completed first. Within a few minutes, I had a massive headache and knew it was time to retake control of the discussion.

"Stop!" I called out. "This isn't getting us anywhere. We can't have everyone advocating their ideas all at once and trying to make them heard above the crowd. We need a different approach and I have one I'd like to recommend. It's called multi-voting. The way it works is that each of you gets four votes. You can use them any way you like. You can cast all your votes for one of the initiatives or spread them around any way you see fit. In this way, we will quickly see what is important to the group as a whole. We can then prioritize our efforts. One thing is for sure — we can't work on everything at once! I have a different color marker for each of you to use. Just walk up to the flip chart. With your marker, make an 'X" or any other symbol you wish to indicate your votes."

During the prior discussion, I listed all our initiatives on the flip chart, so the team was ready to vote. This process took some time to complete as people carefully considered which initiatives they felt were important. In the end, the results indicated some clear priorities.

The Three Ps	Topic	Votes
Production	Obtain the contract.	5
	Convert Line #1 to Epsilon.	6
	Develop Line #2 to run all products.	0
	Set up Line #3 and 4 for all products except Epsilon.	3
Performance	PM	4
	PdM	1
	Reliability repairs	6
	RCFA	1
People	Teams	1
	Communication	5

As everyone looked over the results, I heard many interesting comments about our top five items. One thing that jumped out at us concerned the initiative of obtaining the Epsilon contract — it was not a true initiative at all. In fact, it resulted from successfully accomplishing the other high-scoring initiatives that were the real drivers of our success. In other words, a case could be made that converting Line #1 to Epsilon, creating a reliability repair strategy, developing and implementing a PM program, and improving communication and involvement, would get us the Epsilon contract in the end.

Among the questions, the most helpful to the team was from Dani. She couldn't understand why obtaining the contract wasn't an initiative. I think my explanation helped the group to understand the process better — that any initiative which has other initiatives as its activities is not really an initiative. Instead, it is an outcome of doing the work.

Our next step was to develop activities for the four key initiatives. We brainstormed, using the same process we had used earlier when developing our initial goal list. This time, however, it was easier because a task-focused group such as ours really had no problem developing a task list.

At the end of the day we had develop a detailed activity list for each of the initiatives. I have summarized the activities rather than list all the detail. My purpose is to provide you with an overview of the activities we planned. I have also listed the names of the team members who volunteered to handle each initiative.

Initiative	Activity
Convert Line #1 to Epsilon. (entire team)	Determine changes required to convert the line to Epsilon. Develop a check list and work plan for the conversion process. Identify, develop, and conduct training for operations and maintenance. Identify and address raw material feed issues. Identify and address end product shipping and handling issues. Address safety and environmental issues.
Reliability-based repairs (Nick and Pete)	Create detailed work plans including analysis of failures. Develop and execute per defined work schedules. Take a systems approach to repairs instead of just addressing individual pieces of equipment. Develop a reliability work process.
PM (Gene and Sally)	Identify equipment to receive PM. Identify equipment types and frequency. Identify and deploy the PM process. Develop a process to maximize uptime.
Communication (Dani, Pat, and Lois)	Weekly newsletter Town meetings Promote the ATP3Co vision. Create a feedback process so that we know if our communications are effective.

Last but not the least, part of the process covered the measures that were needed to identify completion of each activity and the associated time frame. As we were discussing this topic, Pat tried to get the group to develop detailed plant performance measures, not measures of the activities as I had instructed the team. I had explained the goal achievement model at a prior meeting. However, Pat was probably worried about the upcoming discussion with Allen and was looking for some ideas to placate him

I stopped him in mid-sentence. "Pat," I said. "As much as we need to measure some of the things you mention, they are not part of the goal achievement model. What we need to measure here are the activities themselves; otherwise, we may never get them completed." That brought Pat back to reality and we were able to move forward. Rather than assign individual measures to individual team members, it made more sense to let the initiative sub-teams figure out the timing and how to measure their success. These sub-teams already had been set up and this approach seemed like the most logical one.

The team meeting ended at about 1:30, giving Pat and me time to get ready for the teleconference with Allen. We had e-mailed our work plan to his office so that he could review it before the meeting and be able to ask any questions. I was worried. Allen was the role model for Mike Kane's and Doug McDonald's reactive mentality. His approach was pure task thinking. It didn't leave a lot of room for a strategic approach. I'll grant you that Allen was a successful businessman. Over the last twenty years, he turned his company into a major player in the tractium business.

However, the world of business is extremely dynamic. Neither a person nor a business can survive without proactively changing to meet new market directions. Epsilon was that new direction. If Allen wasn't going to allow us to change, we — all of us — were going to be in trouble. I believed that Pat and I could succeed in making the Eastern plant reliable, be able to produce Epsilon, and win the contract if we could get Allen to change, but I wasn't sure how we were going to do that. I also wasn't sure if the chart showing how we were planning to convert Line #1 would be detailed enough to satisfy Allen.

At the appointed time the phone rang and Pat answered. As always, Allen got right to the point. "Pat, Todd – I looked over the plan you sent me and I'm very disappointed. I expected a work plan but I wanted much more detail. In other words, specifically how are you going to accomplish what you only superficially outlined? Explain to me how you're going to handle this project so we can discuss your ideas, and I can tell you where the gaps are in the plan."

I looked over at Pat who had slumped down in his chair. He looked like he was trying to hide. The look on his face and his body language reminded me of a child waiting to be reprimanded by a parent. My guess was that he was going to provide little help.

"Allen," I said. The plan seems high level because we have teams working on both the conversion of Line #1 to Epsilon and our reliability plan. We want to pull both of these efforts together to win us the contract as well as making the plant more reliable for all future initiatives. As you can see, we have 75 days including weekends if we need them to make this a success. Both Pat and I believe we're on the right course and believe we will be successful. Our plan is to keep the pressure on the teams and, of course, communicate the high-level status to you weekly."

"Todd that is totally insufficient. I want the details and I want the status of each of the detailed items at what now is going to be a daily teleconference with me. From now on, I control this effort. I've made this company a success to this point and will continue to do so. Understand?"

I was in shock, but the source of Doug and Mike's management style was now crystal clear. Allen was the real role model; his managers were just emulating a behavior that apparently had made Allen and them successful within ATPCo. I knew we were in real trouble. My Western plant experience with Doug and my recent experience with Mike all came flooding back to me. I also knew that without some drastic action, all, and I mean all, was lost. So I did something that was totally unexpected for me, for Pat, and certainly for Allen. I hung up the phone on the president of the company.

Pat flew up from his chair. "Todd, do you know what you just did? You just hung up on Allen! He's going to call back in a minute and if you think he was angry before, I can guarantee you that he's going to be even angrier now. Your career's finished and you have probably taken me down with you. Thanks a lot for nothing!"

"Listen, Pat. If you think about it for a minute, Allen's solution will be the ruin of us all. He has no idea of how to proceed. It's going to be just like Mike and the Line #3 belt failures. Except this time, the machine won't be the only thing that fails. It will be the entire company, our jobs, and the jobs of all those people we talked to the other day and convinced were working at the new ATP3Co."

"So what are we going to do?" Pat asked. "I certainly don't have any idea and right now I wish Mike was back and I was simply back running Line #1."

"Pat, I think we both can agree that if Allen has his way, we're finished." Pat sank back down in his chair and nodded; clearly he agreed. It actually seemed that he was resigned to his fate — a rather unpleasant one at that. On the other hand, I had a different idea about how my fate was going to unfold and, I hoped, the fate of Eastern plant as well.

I paged Lois and asked her to have the steering team come to Pat's office right away. I also told her to put Allen on hold when he called back. I wanted the team assembled first. I explained to her the urgency of the situation and asked her to get them together as quickly as possible. Within a few minutes, Allen called. Lois reluctantly put him on hold over his protest. From the look on her face, I expected he was far more than just angry at what had just happened.

It wasn't much longer before the entire steering team arrived at the office. "Folks, Allen is on hold. All Pat and I want you to do is listen. Please no comments during this discussion. You'll see in a minute how important this is to all of us, our co-workers, and the company. Again please no comments."

I hit the on button and said, "Hello, Allen. Sorry for the interruption, but Pat and I needed to talk before we responded to your plan. Allen, I've assembled our steering team in Pat's office so that they can listen to this discussion. The outcome may lead to our successfully getting the contract and ultimately becoming the industry leader in the tractium production business or it will lead to our collective demise.

"Your plan detailing steps to achieve our goal in the next 75 days won't work. This is not a tactical exercise like repairing a broken pump. This is a strategic work initiative about first becoming a reliability-based plant and, as a result, winning the tractium contract. Working this as a tactical exercise and reporting to you daily so you can redirect our efforts is a waste of your time and everyone else's as well. In addition, it doesn't allow us to use the intelligence and knowledge we all have about the business — the very reason you hired us.

So here's my plan. We will proceed as we have started and keep you informed weekly and more frequently as we get closer to the site visit. But you're not going to interfere with the process because I believe if you do we will fail, not only to get the contract but also we may be out of business as well."

There was a long silence on the line. I wasn't sure what the outcome of what I had just said was going to be. I had just reprimanded the president of the company. The faces of the steering team members ran from shock to disbelief and total surprise. It was clearly written on all their faces.

Then Allen cleared his throat. "Todd, Doug was right about you. You have one hell of a nerve! Whether you believe it or not, I know better than you do how to run this company. My problem is that you and Pat are all I've got right now. My other managers are unavailable and I have some extremely sensitive and highly important things going on or I would come out there and take over this effort. But I can't, so for now keep the chart as it is and we'll talk again in a week. Keep working with your team as you have been, but don't let me down or you will be sorry beyond your wildest dreams!" With that he hung up, or should I say slammed his phone down.

Everyone began speaking at once. Gene was able to make himself heard over the racket. "Todd," he asked as everyone quieted down, "what were we going to do if Allen had persisted with his plan?"

"Pat and I were going to tell Allen we quit," I said. "It would have been my one last ditch effort to save everything and it would have been worth it."

"That would have been interesting," Gene said smiling. I knew he knew where I was going with the discussion and nothing more was needed to be said.

"I'll see you all tomorrow and we can start planning how to convert Line #1. Remember folks, it's my way or the highway," I said laughingly as I raise my left hand with three fingers extended. There was a new role model in the Eastern plant.

CHAPTER 10

THERE ARE OUTCOMES AND IMPACTS FOR EVERYTHING

By the time I got back to my office following the teleconference with Allen, I was exhausted. It is not every day that you get to stick your neck way out with the very likely chance that someone is going to chop off your head. In the back of my mind, I hadn't thought Allen would have fired me. I really did believe Pat and I were his only hope, but you never know. I had thought that

Doug had no options either, yet he transferred me all the way across the country. After all, Allen could have simply fired me and taken over the effort through Pat. I'm sure that he even had other alternatives. But at the time I wasn't thinking about them.

What I was thinking about was Pat, the other members of our steering team, and everyone in the plant. They had taken their first steps toward long-term improvement. I couldn't let all of them down. I couldn't let Allen and his reactive management style destroy all we had started. Therefore, my reaction at the time was — in my opinion — the only right thing to do. The stress of the confrontation had tired me out. I needed some rest, but more than that I felt I needed to communicate with TAN. A lot had happened since our last e-mail exchange several days ago when he had instructed me how to use the goal achievement model.

There were no new e-mails from TAN so I wrote one explaining our initial work with the goal model, my development effort, and the subsequent work by the team building our initiatives and activities. I also explained what had happened with Allen in order to protect our work effort. I even described what had happened with Line #3 and the transposed stock code. I added the information about Line #3 because I was proud of that effort; progress was achieved based on my reliability knowledge and without having to ask TAN for help.

Not expecting an immediate response, I started my day-to-day paperwork. My phone light went on, indicating a waiting voicemail. It was from Allie Thompson, left earlier that afternoon.

"Todd this is Allie. I know I told you that the search could take several months. No, I am not calling to tell you I've found TAN. However, I can tell you that some friends who moonlight for me on special projects have located the geographical area where the e-mails are originating. I don't know if you know anyone out on the West Coast, but I can assure you that the e-mails appear to originate there. I can't be more specific yet, but I'm working on it. You don't need to contact me unless you have questions. I'll be in touch as I get more information."

Well, that was certainly interesting. The trouble was I didn't really know anyone other than my former co-workers at the Western plant, Doug, Allen, and some acquaintances with whom Susan and I had socialized. Other than that, my mind was a blank. At least I knew it wasn't any ATPCo people from the Western plant. They were not TAN-type people.

Just as I was returning to my backlog, I saw that I had received an e-mail from TAN.

```
To: Todd Bradley
From: TAN

I like what you have done with
your goal achievement model. You
are clearly on the right track.
Two things to consider as you
and your team move forward.
First, many initiatives and
their associated activities may
seem somewhat independent, but
are in fact linked. They can't
be addressed as separate compo-
nents of the overall goal
achievement model. If you and
```

your team look closely at the
four initiatives you selected,
you'll see this reality emerge.
Consequently, the sub-teams you
have working on these initiatives need to stay closely connected. Otherwise, you may find
that the different sub-groups
are working at odds with one
another. Have the team think
about this the next time they
get back together.

Second, take time at your team
meeting to carefully examine
both the outcomes from what you
are doing and their impacts.
Your expressed goal must be to
deliver positive impacts for
everyone. Otherwise, the effort
will be undermined by those who
feel they've been negatively
impacted as a result of your
efforts. Carefully consider the
quad diagram I sent you in one
of my last e-mails; the diagram
summarizes this problem.
Like everything else, addressing
outcomes and impacts needs a
structured approach if it is to
be successful. For each outcome
where you have identified a negative impact, try answering
these questions. They will help
you focus on turning negative
impacts to positive ones.

1. What is the negative impact you are trying to correct?
2. Who is impacted?
3. How are you going to correct it? What is the corrective action plan?
4. Who needs to develop the corrective action plan?
5. Who needs to support the corrective action?
6. How will you communicate the corrective action and to whom?
7. How will you audit what you have put into place to make sure it is working?

I also would like to comment about your interchange with Allen. I think what you did was rather drastic. However, with that said, it seems to me that you did the right thing. As you said in your e-mail to me, it is now fairly obvious who trained Doug and Mike — their role model, your leader Allen Peters. Just be careful how often you stick your neck out and make sure it's for the right reason. In this case, I think it was the right reason. I commend you for your quick thinking and action.

I was tired and it was time to go home. I was happy that we had protected our effort to become more reliable from Allen . Most of all, I was happy to be getting out of work at a decent hour, early enough to pick up Susan and take her to a nice restaurant for dinner. She'd been very patient and supportive of my efforts and late-night activities during the two weeks since Mike's death. She clearly deserved a good meal and some quality time with me.

The next morning as I walked through the plant, I noticed something was different. People I hardly knew came up to me to shake my hand. I got a lot more smiles and "good mornings" than I would normally get during one of my plant walk-through tours. I shouldn't have been surprised that the events of the previous afternoon with Allen had been communicated throughout the plant. After all, that was why I had the steering team come to the office before I talked to Allen the second time. I wanted them to see how serious Pat and I were about succeeding in our effort to make the plant more reliable. I knew the word would spread. After all, Dani was the biggest gossip in the plant; I wanted to use the cultural infrastructure to get the message out informally. Of course, the outcome could have been different. The message could have been how Todd committed job suicide in front of his work team. Fortunately this was not the case.

Thinking about what happened the previous day made me think a lot about what TAN had taught me about changing the culture. Pat and I had impacted ATPCo's Eastern plant culture in many ways. We had started to establish the values we wanted to have in place. We had done that both during the teleconference and with the steering team while conducting the root cause failure analysis for Line #3.

Vision:

We will operate our plant so that equipment never fails in an unplanned fashion. This high level of reliability will enable us to continually supply the demands of our customers as well as take on new ones. We will perform this work in a way that recognizes the important and unique value that each person brings to the effort.

Goals	Initiatives	Activities
Production. Operate the equipment properly to consistently meet customer's demand.	1. Convert line #1 to Epsilon production.	Determine changes required to convert the line to the Epsilon process. Develop a detailed work plan and checklist for the process. Set up a work team with no other focus than this job. Develop and conduct training for operators and maintenance as required. Identify and address any raw material or end product issues. Address safety and environmental issues.
Performance. Maintain and operate the equipment in a reliable manner at all times.	1. Implement a reliability-focused repair process. 2. Institute a PM program	Create detailed work plans with a reliability focus instead of a "quick fix." Develop weekly work schedules and follow them. Make repairs focused on the system, not just the specific piece of equipment. Create best practices for work crews to follow to assure reliability-based repairs take place. Identify equipment to receive PM; include frequency and work scope. Set up the process and track compliance. Incorporate a way to maximize PM but minimize downtime.
People. Treat all people as a critical part of the team with dignity and respect.	1. Communicate via forums and other means.	Set up the following: weekly newsletter, monthly town meeting, and a feedback process. Promote ATP3Co concept (also the three fingers).

Furthermore, we had taken a significant step in altering the site's role models. Pat and I had replaced Mike. Surely Mike Kane's presence was still felt, but not as much as before Pat and I started introducing changes. We also had another achievement: creating several new stories for the storytellers. I hoped the recent events would replace the Mike Kane stories with new stories of commitment to the reliability-focused work culture.

The steering team was eager to get started. They clearly were energized from yesterday. Our first task was to agree on the finalized goal achievement model. Maybe because of the prevailing mood, getting everyone to agree was simpler than I had expected. I have provided the working version on the opposite page; this version excludes the initiatives that we had put on hold for now. As we had agreed, each sub team would focus on their individual items. However, converting Line #1 to Epsilon was so important that we all agreed to work on it together.

I still had TAN's comments in mind about how it was very likely that all the four initiatives fit together somehow. The team had performed well the previous day. However, learning the goal achievement model would take time. With that in mind, I wasn't sure how to explain to them that the initiatives were independent efforts yet they were also dependent on one another.

I was saved from this task when Sally, who is normally quiet and never asked a question, said, "I can see how the elements, our initiatives if you will, each need to be worked separately. But don't many, maybe all of them, have linkages to each other? I mean, after all, if we convert Line #1 to Epsilon aren't we going to have to do it in a way that the line can be operated reliably? Not only that, but doesn't PM and even the reliability work process support the Line #1 conversion as well? What I'm saying is that each piece, although separate, needs to be a part of our discussion about converting Line #1."

"That's true," said Pete, "but we also need to take into account that developing a plant-wide reliability process goes beyond just Line #1. It needs to be applied across the other lines as well."

"So," I chimed in, very much relieved and pleased that someone else had verbalized TAN's idea, "we agree that while the sub-teams are working on their individual pieces, they also need to be tightly linked to our current main objective — which is to convert Line #1."

Again I was surprised when Lois, who Pat and I only brought in to take notes said, "That also applies to our communications approach. We can't just wait until we are done doing whatever we plan. We need to tell everyone as we go along, so that they will feel part of the ongoing effort." When she was done she looked embarrassed; almost as if she had spoken out of turn.

Gene broke a brief silence by saying, "Great job, Lois. I couldn't agree with you more. I hadn't thought about that until you brought it up."

I knew he had thought about it before, but his comment really had Lois beaming. "OK, everyone," I said. "I think we all agree that our initiatives are dependent and independent at the same time. We need to work on them in this manner, but we also need to move on. We need to examine our activities and determine how long we need to convert Line #1 and begin producing Epsilon. We also need to assign someone the responsibility for working with all of the departments to coordinate the effort."

Fortunately we had many of the functional leaders as part of our steering team. Distributing the tasks wasn't as hard as it could have been without their presence. The way we split up the work was as follows:

- Determining the necessary changes to the line: Sally due to her background and her role as engineering manager
- Developing the detailed work plan: Pete as operations manager along with Nick, based on his maintenance background
- Setting up the work team: I took that one because I thought Owen McKee was the person for the job. He was currently my maintenance superintendent and I had been told that he had also spent many years in operations as well.
- Developing the training: Dani and Gene, at least the operations portion. I mentioned that they were going to have to work with Sally as the line conversion needs emerged, because that was what needed to be conveyed to the operators. Nick was assigned to develop the maintenance training.
- Product supply and distribution: Pat was assigned, or should I say volunteered, to handle. His role as plant manager would make it easier to get this type of information from the supply and distribution groups within corporate.
- Safety and environmental issues: We left these alone, expecting that they would be handled as the team did the work to prepare Line #1 for con version. If not, we could address them as the issues emerged in this area.

It was lunch time. Everyone was ready to get something to eat and return to work, but we weren't exactly done yet. "Folks, I agree that we have identified our activities and I can clearly see that you are ready to dig right in. But there is one more thing we still need to do. We need to examine the outcomes of what we are doing and their impacts. We need to assure ourselves that all potential negative impacts are addressed and converted to positive ones. So, get some lunch and let's get back together in one hour."

They were excited about the work that we were about to undertake. I was as well, but as I walked back to my office I felt depression coming on. Even though I was pleased with what we had done so far; the real work was just beginning. Maybe the enormity of the task before us was the reason I felt this way, or maybe it was the fear of failing to obtain the Epsilon contract.

I didn't know what I needed to do to get past this feeling and clear my head before we reconvened in the afternoon. I could have called Susan, but although she would try to help she wouldn't understand what was going on at a business level. My only answer was TAN. I returned to my office and sent him an e-mail explaining how I felt, asking if he could help me get past it. I wasn't looking for a cure, just some insight and understanding about what was happening to me. I didn't expect an answer right away and was, therefore, thoroughly surprised when I received a response in less than ten minutes.

To: Todd Bradley
From: TAN

Todd, I'm surprised that the feeling you are experiencing took so long to arrive. What you

are feeling is a perfectly normal response. I'll try to
explain it to you using the following diagram.

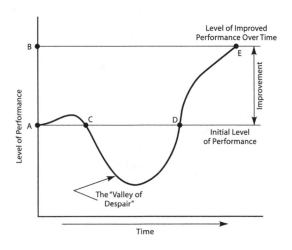

The y-axis is the level of performance. The x-axis is time.
When you started this effort and
we started corresponding, you
were at point A. The horizontal
line from point A was your current and less-than-acceptable
level of performance. Where you
want to be is at the higher performance level indicated by the
horizontal line drawn from point
B. The line from A through C and
D that ultimately gets you to
point E is the path that you,
your steering team, and everyone
at the plant need to follow to
get there.

The temporary increase in performance from A to C is what all
of you have been experiencing.
It was evident at your town
meeting, your success with Line
#3, and the initial development
of the goal achievement model.
Now, however, you — and I mean
you alone — have passed point C
and are starting to understand
the difficulty of the work that
lies before you. That decrease
in performance, along with what
you are feeling, has arrived
because you are in what we call
the "Valley of Despair."
Fortunately for your team, you
arrived first. Once you figure
out how to get through the valley, you will be able to guide
your team when they too arrive.
And believe me, they will be
here shortly.

The path from point C to D is
difficult for anyone. It's even
more difficult for you because
you have far less time than most
organizations trying to change.
The only two pieces of advice I
can offer you are these. First,
keep to your plan. The goal
achievement model, if applied,
will not let you down. Second,
tackle the work in planned seg-
ments, according to the model.

> If you don't approach the change
> effort in planned segments, you
> and the team will quickly get
> overwhelmed. Just remember you
> can't do everything at once.
> Follow both of these pieces of
> advice and I guarantee you will
> reach your goal.

What TAN wrote made perfect sense. It was up to me to serve as a guide and lead my team through the Valley of Despair. I wished I had more time to think about it, but everyone was returning from lunch. Understanding the outcomes and impacts of our efforts awaited us.

I kicked off the afternoon meeting by describing for the team the importance of a detailed examination of the outcomes and impacts that result from completed activities. I explained that every activity had related outcomes and these outcomes had positive as well as potentially negative impacts on the plant personnel. We then worked as a group to identify the outcomes and what we believed could be negative impacts. Any negative impacts would need to be addressed and mitigated. Some of the outcomes identified by the team were not specific enough for our analysis; these were shelved for future development and discussion.

In the end we focused ourselves on the three outcomes that we thought we needed to address. There were probably others that had merit as well. But we identified these three as especially important and agreed to address the others as they emerged. I was willing to live with this solution. I thought that if we identified the major outcomes with potential negative impacts, the team could subsequently tackle the others using their continually developing skills in this area.

The three outcomes we identified were 1) the need for increased training of the workforce to be able to run Epsilon, 2) the need to keep the equipment running reliably, and 3) the requirement that each and every one of us change our work habits. Each of these outcomes had associated with it potentially negative impacts which we had to consider and address.

> 1. We needed to conduct a lot of training but we had little experience. With Epsilon being run on Line #1, the need for additional training of both operators and maintenance mechanics was critical. If we couldn't provide proper training, it would be impossible to keep the line repaired or permit the operators to perform their job adequately — a serious negative impact on all of us.

> 2. With Line #1 exclusively producing Epsilon, the other lines would need to be more flexible and reliable if we were to be able to produce Alpha, Beta, Cappa, and Delta to meet our contractual commitments. We needed to make certain that our reliability efforts didn't fail or the negative impact would be disastrous.

> 3. Last but not least, everyone would have to change the way they worked and, even more so, the way they thought about equipment reliability. Failure to change our mindset would result in serious problems and a failure to achieve our initiatives, goals, and ultimately our vision. We needed to have people who understood the importance of proactively keeping the lines operational. The impact of not making this change would be to slip back

into the Mike Kane mode of operation, with disastrous results.

The first two outcomes — training and reliability — were already included in our other initiatives or in activities associated with Line #1's conversion. Number three was different and needed to be addressed. Many of us in the room understood that there were still people in our plant at many levels in the organization who liked the Mike Kane mode of operation — rapid response to real or perceived emergencies and instantaneous reward, the old "pat on the back."

Before we could rush off and begin planning the Line #1 conversion, we needed to address the Mike Kane mindset that still existed within the plant because it had the potential to ruin our efforts. Therefore, I introduced TAN's corrective action checklists. Of course, I didn't tell the team how I acquired the list. I just indicated that there was a list I had available to help us work through this issue. Fortunately no one asked where I got it. Working through the check list took the rest of the afternoon, but it was well worth the effort. The results and how we planned both to identify and to correct our people problems as they emerged.

- **What is the negative impact we wish to correct?**

  People are not willing to change and, as a result, the effort is undermined.

- **Who is impacted?**

  Everyone

- **How are we going to correct it?**

  First we have to identify the problem. When we recognize it, we need to work with those involved to understand why they refuse to change. We can then help them to understand the value for everyone if they do.

- **Who needs to develop the corrective action plan?**
  The steering team
- **Who needs to support the action?**
  Everyone on site needs to recognize and support the change as the new way we do our business. Those who don't support it are hampering our ability to change the way we work. Everyone needs to have this mindset.
- **How will we communicate the corrective action and to whom?**
  Use communication initiatives such as town meetings, etc.
- **How will we audit that the new work culture we have in place is working?**
  The work culture and overall mode of operations will change. If we pay careful attention, these changes should be fairly obvious.

Everyone had their assignments. As we broke up for the day I could tell that they were ready to get to work. Our focus was to convert Line #1 to Epsilon as well as accomplish all of the associated initiatives and their activities. There were only two days left in the week so we agreed to work on our assignments and reconvene Monday. Everyone actually planned mini meetings because in the end everything was really linked together.

I still had one task to complete before I could end my day. I need to recruit Owen to lead the Line #1 conversion effort. I hadn't spent much time with him in the last several weeks, having been preoccupied with developing the steering team and moving our effort forward. Still, I was certain he was the right person for the job. I had asked him to meet me at my office at the end of the day. When I arrived, he was already waiting for me.

We talked about plant operations, which seemed to be reliable — at least reliable for the moment. We also discussed some of the gossip related to my conversation with Allen. Before moving on, I explained to Owen what had happened and how Allen had agreed to let us continue. Then I got to the point. "Owen, I want you to lead the line conversion effort. The steering team members — you know who they are — are working on various aspects of the plan. However, we need someone with your experience to pull all of the conversion efforts together. I know you have the maintenance background and I just learned from Pat you have extensive operating experience as well. So, you are the person I want for the job. What do you say?"

Owen was pleased. I could tell from his face that he was also excited about being given the opportunity. He accepted enthusiastically. We spent the next hour discussing his role. I was very specific that he was to focus on the line conversion and nothing else. His efforts also included coordinating the work team from maintenance that would be assigned to the conversion. We both understood that moving so many mechanics to Line #1 would shortchange the other lines, but the conversion project was very important.

When we were done, Owen left to see if he could find any of the steering team members to speak with so he could get a deeper understanding of his role. I didn't expect him to find anyone because it was already after hours. Another long day was over and it was time for me to go home.

On my way out, I noticed that the light in the conference room was still on. Being an energy-conscious person, I went over to shut it off. To my astonishment, the entire steering team and Owen were there discussing the Line #1 conversion plan. Not wanting to miss out on all the fun, I put my briefcase down and joined in. I also remembered to call Susan and tell her that I was staying for another long evening. As always, she understood and surprised us all when she had dinner delivered!

CHAPTER 11

I ADDRESS RESISTANCE

We estimated that the work preparation phase, which was ultimately developed by the team for Line #1, would take two weeks. It included engineering, operational, and maintenance changes along with training. It also included some minor changes related to line supply and packaging of the end product. In addition to the two weeks of preparation, we estimated that the actual conversion would take another week, during which time the line would actually be down. We also had weekends and overtime available on an as-needed basis to address any unexpected issues that arose. Everyone had worked hard to develop the plan, even to the point of working part of the weekend so that it would be ready for the steering team review meeting Monday morning.

By now Owen had taken on the role of the lead for the effort. At our Monday meeting, he took everyone through each of the steps of the process, both the two-week preparation phase and the actual conversion work. The work plan covered all of the aspects that we had discussed previously as well as our goal achievement model. He presented some other ideas that I didn't remember discussing previously with the team. One of the key ideas dealt with developing our PM program. I had thought we would address this topic at a later date — after we had completed the line conversion. However, some members of the steering team had been discussing our conversion effort with the line operators and the maintenance crews assigned to the Line #1 project.

At some point in the discussion, the goal achievement model was described. I guess it was only natural curiosity that kept the discussion going, but at some point, blending PM with line shutdowns came up. An important fact about the tractium lines is that they don't run continuously, even though we would like them to operate in this fashion. The truth is that quite often they need to be shut down for feed changes, packaging changes, or even minor line adjustment. These periods of downtime can run from 15 minutes (a single adjustment) all the way to a feed change that takes several hours.

The operations and maintenance ad-hoc team suggested that we plan the PM or adjustments in great detail, then take advantage of these line outages to do the work. They even created a name for this process: Line Down PM. In this way, the work would get done without any effect on the run time of the equipment. They even went far beyond simply suggesting the idea; they developed detailed plans for the various efforts. This idea was so good and so simple that many questioned why this was never done before.

Everyone loved the concept, so we set up a subteam from those who had developed the idea. The subteam would build some scenarios that could be tested during outages that occurred before the conversion. In this way, we believed we would see if the concept would work and, if it did, we could fully incorporate it into our overall plan. We also liked the concept because it helped us achieve a performance initiative in the goal achievement model.

In the end, with very little discussion, the work plan was adopted. The Line Down PM concept was also tentatively adopted pending the test scenarios that we were going to run during the normal line-down situations. Within a few days we had several opportunities to test the concept. While the line was down for a packaging alteration of 30 minutes, the maintenance mechanics were ready. They completed a significant amount of planned adjustments, many of which had not been made for a long time. One time when the line was shut down for a feed change, maintenance had been advised of the event's timing and was able to replace a motor that had been causing operations a problem. There were several other outages with associated PM, all of which had been planned in great detail. These maintenance efforts were carried off without a hitch and with no delay in restarting the equipment. As many of us knew it would, the Line Down concept worked and was subsequently incorporated into our line conversion plan. The best part of the whole event was that the idea had been created by the workforce with minimal help from the steering team. This fact was significant because previously these same workers would have been afraid to even suggest a better way to do something than the Mike Kane way. We felt so good about this accomplishment that we took all of those involved and their significant others out to dinner at the best restaurant in town.

This new concept of conducting PM while the line was down inspired another benefit that was totally unexpected. We had assigned communications to Dani and Lois. I assumed they would pursue either another town meeting or some form of memo. I was wrong. At the end of the week, I came into my office to find a single sheet of paper on my chair. It was divided into two columns like a newspaper and at the very top was the title The Tractium Times. Dani and Lois had recognized that town meetings, although useful, required more time than we had available to provide the level of detail needed to keep the workforce properly informed.

I was impressed that someone would think of sending out this form of "one time" communication. It was a novel way to communicate to the plant population. But I was wrong again. Underneath the title were the words, "published weekly for the Eastern Plant of ATP3Co." I also didn't miss the number three following the letter P in the title. Now I was really impressed. Before my plant morning tour, I skimmed *The Tractium Times*. It described in a very succinct format our goal achievement model process, our goals and initiatives, and the Line #1 conversion process. It also gave specific recognition to the operators and mechanics who developed the Line Down PM program.

With a smile on my face, I made my morning rounds and headed for the steering team meeting. This meeting, which had once been focused on developing our goal achievement model, was now focused on a daily review of our progress on the Line #1 conversion. The actual conversion was now less than two weeks away.

Today, rather than having Owen launch into the status report, I asked him to give me a few minutes. "I just wanted to start the meeting by acknowledging Dani and Lois for the work that they have done with *The Tractium Times.* I had never thought about a communication tool like this one. Dani, Lois, you both should be really pleased with what you have developed. Now the difficult part is keeping it going with enough items to keep everyone interested." Dani and Lois beamed as they accepted the congratulations from the team. "One more thing," I said. "We still need to have town meetings just so we can get everyone together and answer questions for the plant personnel."

"Don't worry," Lois said. "You obviously like the format but you didn't read all the information."

"That's true," I admitted.

"If you had, you would have noticed that you and Pat are holding another town meeting towards the end of next week, right before we begin the actual Line #1 conversion. One more thing," Lois said, "Todd you're buying everyone lunch."

All I could do was laugh as I turned the meeting

over to Owen to begin his status report. I was still thinking about *The Tractium Times* and only half listening when something Owen said caught my interest. Operations was on schedule, but maintenance was only at 35% complete with half of the time passed. I wasn't ready to ask any detailed questions yet because no one else seemed to get upset with Owen's explanation and assurance that maintenance would get caught up. I did ask why this trend had not been reported before. Owen had always reported that maintenance was on schedule. He told me that it was just a minor issue that had come to his attention.

My maintenance experience told me that he wasn't being completely truthful. The maintenance effort was behind and regardless of what the other steering team members thought, we were heading into trouble. When the meeting broke up, I decided to get to the bottom of the problem. The easiest way to do that was to go out to the line, observe the work, and talk to the mechanics.

When I got to Line #1, part of the problem was obvious. The work wasn't getting done because the maintenance mechanics were not there. The operators told me that there was an emergency on Line #2 and that Owen had sent them over to fix it. To say the least, I was upset but I wanted to give Owen a fair chance. I walked over to Line #2 to see what the emergency was that reassigned mechanics who were supposed to be dedicated to preparing Line #1 for conversion.

When I arrived at Line#2, I saw Jonah and Jacob working to replace a motor on one of the water pumps. I knew that the pump had a backup, which seemed to be working fine. Rather than jump to conclusions, however,

I looked up Dave, the line supervisor, to get any details I may have missed. "Dave, could you tell me why you called in the water pump as an emergency? Isn't there a backup that should allow you to run without interruption until you can arrange for a replacement?"

"Well, I guess there is, but I thought what if the backup failed? Then we would be shut down and I know management isn't happy when that happens."

"But isn't the backup working okay?" I asked.

"Sure," Dave responded, "but Owen is a friend. He told me the Line #1 work would be okay and the motor replacement would take only a few hours."

"One last question. Is this a common occurrence?" Dave seemed reluctant to answer this one. I suspect that he thought he would get Owen in trouble. With some prodding, he finally admitted that the crew from Line #1 was frequently diverted. Now I was really mad. Pat, the rest of the steering team, and I were trying to change things. We were desperately trying to get Line #1 converted to Epsilon on schedule. We were also trying to change how the Eastern Plant functioned.

I had specifically told Owen to focus his efforts only on Line #1 and he had agreed. Yet whenever people asked for his help — whether the job was really an emergency or not — he diverted the crews. He was pulling them from a planned, scheduled, and very important job. He was behaving just like he had when Mike ran the plant. I knew that if I confronted him now it wouldn't be good for either of us. I needed to calm down, approach and correct the problem logically, and get the conversion effort back on track. I went to the only place I could get some privacy: my office. When I got there, I found an e-mail waiting from TAN.

To: Todd Bradley
From: TAN

Todd, I hope you have worked your way out of the Valley of Despair. You and your team are on the right track. Let me know if I can help

I was still in a black mood after learning about how Owen had moved the crew and explained all of this in a reply to TAN. His reply was almost immediate; almost as if TAN was just waiting at his PC. I couldn't help but wonder who TAN was but that had to wait for Allie. The e-mail was another long one. Obviously TAN had something he wanted it to teach me.

 To: Todd Bradley
From: TAN

As much as you plan and communicate what you are trying to achieve, not everyone will easily join you and your colleagues on the journey. All along the way, now and in the future, and even after you have been proven successful, you will meet resistance. You may ask why people would resist you when what you are doing makes perfect sense and is the right thing to do. The answer is that they may not agree. It may even be as simple that what you are doing takes them out of their comfort zone.

A comfort zone in the work environment is that familiar place where we feel relaxed and safe while performing our tasks. Changes to the comfort zone or requests to work outside of it cause people to do one of two things. One response is to re-establish the status quo and restore the old boundaries in which they were comfortable. Usually this is done through resistance to changes that alter their comfort zone. The second and more preferred response is to expand their comfort zone and create a new status quo, one in which they feel comfortable.

The problem is that people have different capacities for handling change. Some are not able to expand their comfort zones easily and you get resistance as a result. Now when most managers perceive that resistance is taking place, they think that it is an enemy to be overcome and eliminated. This is absolutely not the case! Resistance is an indication that something is not right within the organization. The workers who are resisting have been removed from their comfort zone, usually as a result of change. Their response is to try to restore the status quo.

Before I can discuss how to address resistance — notice I did NOT say overcome — you need to be able to recognize it when it occurs. Resistance can take on one of four different forms, based on whether those resisting are visibly resisting or doing it behind the scenes and whether the resistance is active or passive. The easiest way to see this is through the quad diagram that I have provided. Let me describe each of the sections for you.

		Active	Passive
Visibility of Resistance	**Hidden**	3 Sabotage (Destruction behind the scenes)	4 Submerge (It looks like I am doing it but I'm not)
	Open	1 Struggle (I will not do it)	2 Submit (I'll do it but poorly at best)
		Active	**Passive**
		Degree of Resistance	

1. Struggle (visible and active). In "struggle" mode, resistance presents itself very forcibly. You ask someone to do something and they tell you, "I will not do it." People resisting in this manner are clearly being forced from their comfort zone. Making a statement of this sort is not standard business practice. In some cases, a struggle occurs if you ask employees to do something that they clearly believe is not safe, a task where they believe that they will get injured.

2. Submit (visible and passive). People who don't feel comfortable resisting actively and openly will instead take a passive approach. In "submit" mode, workers will do what you ask, but they will do it poorly. By this action they hope that you will either stop them from doing the work or you will find someone else to do it. In either case, they will have restored their personal status quo, at least for a while.

Suppose you are converting the maintenance process from being totally reactive to one focused on reliability. Employees who are resisting via the submit mode will do the reliability tasks poorly. In your efforts to demonstrate the value of the new process, you will reassign the tasks to others who will do the work well. The result is that those who are uncomfortable in the reliability-focused world will be spared, at least for the short term.

3. Sabotage (hidden and active). In this mode, people work behind the scenes to destroy what you are trying to create. They feel so threatened that they resort to actions that very well may cost them their jobs. At first you may think it worthwhile to understand this behavior and address it. However, in this case, understanding may not be the right approach. Employees who are caught sabotaging the work need to be dealt with far differently than those engaging in other forms of resistance. They need to be disciplined. Depending on the severity of their actions, that discipline could even be their discharge. This approach may seem harsh, but it certainly addresses the issue for those who remain. Resisting for the right reasons is acceptable, especially when working through the issues leads those workers from resistance to acceptance. But under no circumstances is it acceptable to sabotage the business along the way.

4. Submerge (hidden and passive). This form of resistance manifests itself by appearing on the surface that the work is being done. However, when you look deeper, it becomes painfully apparent that the work is actually not being done. As with the other form of passive resistance (submit), people in the submerge mode, are not willing to move to active resistance, although they are out of their comfort zone. Instead, they hope that when their lack of performance is noticed they will no longer be assigned the work and the problem will go away. Submergence is the more difficult of the two passive types of resistance because, if the leadership is not observant, the resistance goes unnoticed until it is too late.

Todd, you are lucky, you recognized that something was wrong when the plan said maintenance should be 50% complete and they were only at 35%. Suppose that you had not investigated the problem until the end of next week. Any resistance in submerge mode would have really had a severely negative impact on your

conversion preparation. This is
the serious nature of what Owen
and a work crew were doing by
resisting.

Now that you understand the different types of resistance, let
me briefly explain why resistance needs to be addressed, not
overcome. Far too many managers
believe that resistance is like
a blot on the organizational
landscape, that it needs to be
removed. Those who treat it as
such do great harm because they
further alienate those in the
organization who are outside of
the comfort zone and, as a
result, are resisting. The harder that managers try to eliminate the resistance, the more
alienated the workers become
because their feelings and concerns about the changes taking
place are essentially being dismissed.

What you need to do is to take
the time to understand the
resistance and the associated
comfort zone issues being experienced. Once you understand why
the workers are reacting this
way, you can take the time to
help them expand their comfort
zone to include the changes.
Some solutions that help this
process include training, coach-

ing, and simply explaining the
rationale behind the changes
taking place.
Now that you know about resistance and can recognize it, what
are you going to do about Owen
and the Line #1 crew? Punish
him? Or address the problem and
correct it? The choice is yours.

TAN was right once again. I needed to address and resolve Owen's problem for his good and the good of us all. Owen was a good supervisor. I knew that if we had a thorough discussion about the conversion and the over-all changes being implemented, I would understand his concerns and he might understand mine. I needed to have this discussion today so I had Lois arrange for him to come to my office.

Soon afterwards, I heard a knock on my door. "Owen, come on in. There is something we need to talk about related to the Line #1 conversion project."

"Sure, Todd, what's up?"

"Owen, the maintenance portion of our plan is behind schedule. We should be 50% complete. Based on our last team discussion, however, we are only at 35%." Owen began to try to explain, but I cut him off.

"Please don't try to explain the problem. I know what it is — and it isn't exactly the reason you have been providing at our morning status meetings. I know from observing the work effort and talking to the operators that you have been diverting Line #1 resources to the other lines. Some of the jobs were indeed emergencies. But others were not and yet were presented to you as if they were emergencies just to get the resources assigned. When we started this effort, we specifically discussed that you and those assigned to the Line #1 project were not to be diverted, no matter what. And yet you moved them anyway. I would at least like to understand why."

Owen looked like the child caught with his hand in the cookie jar. "Todd, it isn't as simple as it appears on the surface. Of the three people I diverted, Jonah and Jacob actually have friends and family operating Lines #2 and #3. You have to remember that under Mike, rapid response was highly praised. For many of the workers, not having that reinforcement makes them feel like something is missing in their lives. This feeling is doubled when the people praising you for your efforts are family and people you regularly socialize with during off hours. I have to admit; I have good friends on Line #4 and was just trying to help them out. If you're angry, I apologize. I promise it won't happen again."

"Owen, I'm not angry; disappointed yes, but not angry. We are trying to change the culture here and I am more than willing to admit that this isn't something that's done overnight. In fact, when we prepared our goal achievement model and reviewed the outcomes and their potential negative impacts, this problem is one we identified as something we needed to watch for and address.

"You, Jonah, Jacob, and I think George was the other mechanic diverted — all of you are feeling out of your comfort zone. I realize that you're used to immediate praise and recognition after a rapid response to the plant emergencies. So, we have two possible ways to go. One, we can figure out how to expand your comfort zone. We find a way of developing and sticking to a plan

— and then not diverting from it — that doesn't make you uncomfortable. In fact, following and completing the plan should give you and the others as much satisfaction and recognition as you got from the Mike Kane mode of working. Or, we have number two, which is to go back to the way things were done. Which path do you think we are going to follow?"

Owen cleared his throat. I could tell he was nervous, but I also got the impression he was determined to correct this issue between us. "I see your point, Todd, and I agree with you. I promise you that it won't happen again. I want to work with everyone to improve our reliability, but I guess it was too easy to slide back into the old way of working. After all, I worked that way for a lot of years, and the new way is just being introduced. It takes some getting used to and, having others in the crew who reacted the same way that I did, made it even easier to slide back. Todd, I promise you. It won't be repeated."

I was grateful for Owen's approach. I knew how hard it was to change, especially when facing a high degree of peer pressure. Owen and I shook hands and he got up to leave. "Wait a minute, Owen. There's something else I want to share with you. If you think about it, Pat and all the others are not like us. We are reliability and maintenance professionals. Yes, they have goals in this area and, yes, reliability and maintenance are important to the success of our effort.

They still don't have the same focus as we do. They run the lines, handle engineering, or in Pat's case run the plant. But our focus is very different. There is no one else in our department who I trust as much as you, based not only on your experience, but also on the kind of person I know you are. That is why I need you to focus on our Line #1 conversion and complete the work on time. I personally selected you for this and need to count on you to get it done. If we pull this effort off, we will be starting down a path that will be of benefit for all of us — even those who still think the old way is better."

With that I got up and escorted him out. I believed that to some extent I had addressed his concerns and that he was back on track. Knowing Owen, it was also my expectation that he would coach the others and help them expand their comfort zones as well. Well, at least I sincerely hoped so.

For the next several days, I paid close attention to how the maintenance portion of the work was progressing. By the time we had used 80% of our two weeks, maintenance was back on track. I also noticed that the mechanics were working before the start of the work day. When I went home, they were still on the job. Furthermore, I never saw a pay slip for overtime for a single one of them.

The day on which we were to start the week-long conversion of Line #1 finally arrived. You could sense an air of excitement throughout the entire plant. Thanks to *The Tractium Times*, everyone knew what was about to happen. The newsletter had kept everyone up-to-date at every stage of the effort. It seemed that Lois had increased the frequency of publication to daily so that she could keep everyone informed. At this time in our lives, weekly just wasn't enough. In fact, I think that everyone on site knew as much about the plan and its status as I did, which was probably a very good idea. There is absolutely nothing wrong with a good communication plan. Then everyone is aware of the status of the work and can actively support it. In addition, good communication eliminates the cultural infrastructure gossips from spreading misinformation, which causes us to waste our time conducting damage control.

The second town meeting was also a huge success, partly because we provided everyone with a very nice lunch. Our job status and updates related to our goal achievement model were delivered by several of the team members; they were well accepted. It seemed to me that people were beginning to believe that the way work was conducted was indeed different in the Eastern Plant. I actually think the hit of the meeting was a large ATP3Co sign that the team had installed at the plant entrance. I'm not sure Allen would have approved, but Pat was enthusiastic as it was his idea. We would have to deal with Allen some other day, but not today.

Learning and the Dangers of Assumptions

The conversion of Line #1 began on a Monday. We had one full week's worth of work to complete in order to make all of the changes needed so that the line could produce Epsilon. Furthermore, we had a considerable amount of PM work to execute as defined by the Line Down PM plan. Because the line was down for an extended outage, we had an opportunity to undertake a considerable amount of maintenance on the equipment, some of which hadn't been completed for years.

As with all such plans, we naturally ran into some problems, but none that we as a team found insurmountable. Some members of the steering team also pitched in. To my surprise and delight, the operators and maintenance crews worked in a far more harmonious manner than these groups normally do. I guess they all understood what was at stake. By the end of a very long week we were essentially finished. We needed to complete some open items over the weekend, but that extra work was not unexpected.

By Monday morning we were ready for start up. As plant manager, Pat was given the honor of pushing the button and energizing the line. He seemed very happy. After all, we had set up our goal achievement model and executed our short-term goals, initiatives, and activities to convert the line per the plan. Even Allen was happy because in the end we had followed the plan we had provided him and delivered on it. He even sounded happy when we gave him the final status report late Sunday night. However, being Allen, even as he praised us for a job well done, he couldn't help but add, "When will the rest of the work on Line #2 be finished?"

Pat had a short speech prepared. I was impressed. I didn't write this one and, in fact, I hadn't even recommended that he make a speech. He had thought of it entirely on his own. Each day he was developing into a plant manager, and not one like Mike or Doug, but a real strategic, people-oriented manager. Someone I would be pleased to work with in the future.

"Ladies and gentlemen," Pat said to the group. "It

has taken us a long time and a great deal of effort by all of us to get to where we are today. We have survived difficult challenges. Collectively, we have emerged better and wiser from the experience. When our prospective client visits, I know that they will find Line #1 running tractium — Epsilon to be specific. Line #2 will be capable of running Epsilon as well as our other products. And Lines #3 and #4 will be running Alpha, Beta, Cappa, and Delta in a very flexible configuration so we can supply market demand regardless of what it happens to be. We still need a week to commission the line, but I am confident that it will be up and running without any problems. We still have a lot to do so let's start this unit up and get on with it." With that he gave the signal and we started the line.

It did take us five days to commission the line. Most of the problems were the normal start-up ones that kept us from reaching maximum production. By Tuesday, however, we had produced the first Epsilon product and by Friday we were shipping Epsilon. Everyone was quite pleased with what we had accomplished. However, on Friday, at the time when the line was finally at full production, Pat and I called a steering team meeting.

I opened the meeting by asking, "What do the numbers 44 and 31 mean to each of you?" This time they knew the answer: 44 calendar days and 31 work days until the client visits. Knowing this answer was no surprise. Everyone was very aware that our visit was fast approaching and we had not completed our plan yet. That was the bad news.

The good news was that setting up Line #2 wasn't going to be nearly as hard as the Line #1 project. After all, Line #2 already ran all of the products except

Epsilon. All we needed was to make adjustments and install some additional equipment; the line would then be set up to run Epsilon. This effort was different from the one needed to run Epsilon exclusively on Line 1. Line #2 was designed to be a backup to Line #1. It would be able to take on additional demand for Epsilon for a short period if Line #1 couldn't handle the full demand.

Owen had been active during the Line #1 commissioning process, but was not actually helping run Line #1. The steering team had provided such good training for the operators and maintenance mechanics, that Owen wasn't needed. That pleased him immensely and allowed him to dedicate his time, along with Sally from engineering and some of his best mechanics, to develop the plan for Line #2.

At the steering team meeting, we finalized our work plan. The plan was designed to have Line #2 in the position we wanted in two weeks: to be able to run any of our tractium products with minimal changeover time. We included extensive Line Down PM in the plan. We also scheduled the training that would enable the operators to run the line and perform reliability-based repairs. I had been so busy with all these efforts that I hadn't e-mailed TAN since we had brought Line #1 online and started working on Line #2. His e-mail response to my status report was a surprise to me.

 To: Todd Bradley
From: TAN

Todd, I am sure you, the steering team, and everyone at the Eastern Plant are very happy with your accomplishments to date. If you stop now, however, even with your successful pro-duction of Epsilon you become stagnant. Continuous improvement is the name of the game.Identify all that you have learned and figure out what's next. You and the team should consider whether your efforts have been a project or a process.

I'm not referring to the conver-sion of Line #1. That was indeed a project, a work effort that had a definite beginning and a definite ending. No, what I am referring to is your overall effort to change the Eastern Plant from what it was under Mike to what you and Pat are calling the new ATP3Co. If you believe this effort is just a project, then you won't truly succeed.

I don't really believe you feel this way, but I need to raise that question. What I do believe, whether you and the team realize it or not, is that you are dealing with a process — something that has a beginning, but truly no end. If this is true, that the effort is a process with no end, you need to figure out how to conduct continuous improvement. For this, I use a process called spiral learning. The reason for the name is that as you move through time, you are actually in a learning spiral. Here is a diagram of what it looks like.

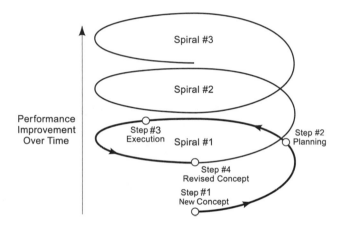

Spiral learning involves a four step process. In Step #1, you identify a new concept, idea, or series of ideas. In Step #2, you plan the work, followed by Step #3 during which you execute the work. At this point, rather than press on in a step-by-step fashion without alteration, you take Step #4. In this step, you review what you have done and learn from it. I can assure you that during the first spiral, you learned many new things, many of which you didn't know

when you started. You then apply
this new information in your
next spiral so that you continuously improve. Using the work
that you have just completed,
consider the difference between
a project, which is a linear
process, and the spiral process
I just described.

In a linear model, you would
have converted Line #1 and then
used the same plan with some
minor alterations to set up Line
#2. Neither learning nor contin-
uous improvement would be fac-
tors when setting up the second
line. Now let's look at what you
have done and see how it fits
the learning spiral concept. At
Step #1 you recognized that you
needed to convert Line #1. You
planned and executed the work in
Steps #2 and #3, but you also
learned along the way. I think
the most significant piece of
learning was the Line Down PM
concept. Forget for a moment
that you actually employed it on
Line #1's conversion. Just consider that at Step #4, when you
reviewed what you learned, you
recognized the new PM concept.
While you applied it with Line
#1, you actually worked it into
the initial planning in the sec-

```
ond spiral, which covered the
conversion of Line #2. Without
spiral learning, the Line Down
PM concept never would have been
applied to Line #2.

Spiral learning also applies to
a higher level, namely the goal
achievement model. You and the
team built that model before you
started Line #1 conversion. Now
it's time to see what you
learned and reapply it to the
next spiral, thereby modifying
to some degree your goal
achievement model.
```

Spiral learning was an interesting concept, one that I certainly hadn't consciously thought about before. I could see how we were already applying the concept to a limited extent. After all, when we started our Line #1 conversion plan, we hadn't applied or even dreamed of Line Down PM. In fact, we created the idea along the way and blended it into our total effort. So in a way we had unknowingly applied spiral learning.

However, TAN's idea of applying the concept to our goal achievement model was new. It seemed like a good idea because it would support our plan for continuous improvement beyond the Line #1 effort. I also remembered the e-mail in which TAN had described group learning, both Type I and Type II. Spiral learning was Type II learning. The more I thought about it, the more I recognized we needed to incorporate spiral learning as part of our master plan. Therefore, I wrote some quick notes and decided to present the idea at our next steering team meeting on Monday.

Today was apparently an e-mail day because, just as I had finished my notes on Type II learning, I got another e-mail. This one was from Allie reporting on her progress. It had been a while since I had last heard from her. Her e-mail told me that she had firmly pinned down TAN's location. It was on the West Coast. The problem was that I didn't know many people out there so most likely TAN was not someone I knew. Allie's message was still good news. She and the people helping her had narrowed the location of TAN to an area east of Los Angeles, almost at the Arizona border.

Once again Allie assured me that her efforts would be successful. However, because of the need for outside support, she needed more money. She promised that an additional $250 would be the limit. She added that regardless of any further costs, I would not need to provide additional funding; she would cover it. I had already invested $1000 in this effort so I wrote out and mailed her the check for the $250. I also sent her an e-mail confirming that the money was on its way.

Our next steering team meeting convened early on Monday. We had gotten into the habit of checking off the days remaining until the site visit so when I asked, "what do 41 and 30 mean to you?" they all already knew the answer.

"Everyone, today we are going to move our process another step forward. We've converted Line #1 and currently are shipping Epsilon. Line #2 work is under way and Owen is dedicating his efforts to completing the conversion by next Friday. So we will have Lines #1 and #2 set up as planned. Lines #3 and #4 have had very few problems since we corrected the belt issue. More work is still needed and we will discuss this shortly. However, what we need to do now is step back so that we can re-examine and upgrade our goal achievement model."

Everyone seemed surprised. Sally was the first to speak up. "Todd, I thought that we were finished with that piece of business. After all we have the vision and goals as well as having identified and completed many of our initiatives and activities."

"True, Sally, but we need to consider a process of continuous improvement. There needs to be life after the visit. Let me introduce a concept to you all and see what you think about it. We all know that group learning is one of the eight elements of change. Typically the way we understand group learning is that we set goals, execute activities, compare the results, identify the gaps, and adjust our activities to get closer and closer until we reach our goals. This model is called Type I learning.

The thing that is missing is that periodically we need to readjust the goals. Why? Because as we progress we learn more, and what we learn needs to be integrated into our goals if we are going to continuously improve. This is often called Spiral Learning because each cycle can be viewed as a spiral in which we plan, execute, learn, and readjust our plans as we move forward.

"Folks, we have used Type I learning as we moved from where we were to our current position — producing Epsilon. Now it is time to move to Type II learning and see if we need to adjust our goals and get better than we already are."

I could see that I had made my point as several

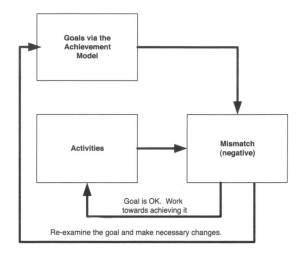

team members voiced agreement. The momentary silence was broken by Nick, who said, "I'm all for this review of the goal achievement model. I've been looking the model over recently and I think we have learned a lot since we first got together. I'd like to review it as a group and, quite frankly, improve upon what we have already developed."

I was ready and handed out our goal achievement model. We shared our normal level of discussion as we prepared to actually dig into the work — a necessary part of group dynamics, even for a team such as ours who had worked together for several weeks. Our meeting lasted into the early evening. In the end, we had made some improvements to the goal achievement model. As a team, we felt we had added the component of continuous improvement it had lacked. In the chart on the next page I've included our original work effort and the status of the initiatives. I've also shown the changes we made in bold so you can see the upgrades. The document doesn't extend to the activities or the

Goal	Initiative
Production. Operate the equipment **in an optimal manner** to consistently meet the customer's demand.	1. Obtain the Epsilon contract. – work in progress 2. Convert Line #1 to Epsilon. – completed 3. Develop Line #2 to run all products. – in progress 4. Operate Lines #3 and #4 in a flexible manner. – done 5. **Understand and incorporate other ATPCo site's best practices into the production process. Be the best site in the company. – new**
Performance. Maintain and operate the equipment in a reliability manner at all times.	1. **Expand the Line Down PM program to handle short, long, and while running PM efforts. – new** 2. **Institute a PdM program to identify failures before they happen. - new** 3. Institute a reliability repair process. 4. **Conduct root-cause failure analysis and perform corrective action on all failures, both major and minor – changed**
People. Treat all people as a critical part of the team with dignity and respect.	1. Employ work teams at the lines and throughout the plant. 2. **Handle communications on a frequent basis in person and by various other means. – changed.** 3. **Expand and modify the steering team to enable employee self-directed activities with steering team oversight. – new.**

examination of outcomes and impacts. That effort was put on hold until we got past the more immediate problem, which was the visit by our prospective customer.

Collectively, the team believed we had done a good job with their rework of the goal achievement model. It was an impressive effort on several levels. We had completed the work in one day compared to how long it would have taken in the past. We clearly had learned from our work over the last 45 days and were able to apply what we had learned. In addition, we had built a plan for continuous improvement. It was clear to me that everyone understood this was going to be an ongoing process, not a project that ended when we were awarded the Epsilon contract. Overall, it was a day well spent.

The next day as I was making my rounds, I noticed something that was more than just disturbing. It set off alarms in my head that told me something serious was wrong. I saw Jonah and Jacob working on Line #3. As with Line #1's conversion, they had been relieved of their regular duties and assigned to the conversion effort for Line #2. Clearly Owen had gone back on his promise and diverted the crew once again. All I could see was red as I made my way back to my office. I closed the door and sank down in my chair. I felt betrayed by someone I trusted. I had trusted Owen with two of the most important efforts we had: the conversion of Lines #1 and #2.

Apparently my good sense must have prevailed because I didn't rush out of the office to confront him right away. Instead, I tried to calm myself down. I took a deep breath and then wrote an e-mail to TAN, explaining my predicament and asking for advice. I was beside myself. I liked Owen and he had really done a good job on Line #1. Furthermore, it looked like he was doing an equally good job on Line #2.

The e-mail from TAN came back rather quickly. At times I was amazed at the rapidity of his responses.

To: Todd Bradley
From: TAN

Todd, I am glad you didn't jump to conclusions and confront Owen until you read what I have to say. You are falling into a trap that could be the undoing of all that you and your team have worked to achieve. You are preparing to act without facts. All you have right now are assumptions about Owen's decisions. I can assure you that assumptions are often wrong; they get people into a great deal of unwanted trouble. If you break the word "assume" apart, what do you get? You get actions that make an "ass of u and me." I don't want that to happen, so read on.

Peter Senge wrote a book called "The Fifth Discipline: The Art and Practice of the Learning Organization." In his book, he described a concept originally developed by Chris Argyris called the Ladder of Inference.

Essentially, the concept describes how we as human beings make judgments based on our experiences. We encounter vast amounts of information every day: written, verbal, and visual. Our minds filter this information and select data and experiences to store. Once stored, we fix meaning to this information and make mental assumptions about all of it. From these assumptions, we draw conclusions and ultimately develop a set of beliefs on which we act. In addition, the next time we process similar data that matches what we have already stored, we react in the same manner.

Let me give you an example from my own experience. As you read this, however, I would ask you to keep in mind your assumption that Owen diverted the crew. Years ago I was a field execution manager for a large petrochemical plant. One summer day I arrived at the job site to check the status of the work. The crew was busy except for one man, I'll call him Ed. He was off to the side, his shirt off, getting a nice suntan. I observed everything going on, but my mental filter focused on Ed. From what

I saw, everyone was working except lazy old Ed. I assumed that he was resting while letting the rest of the crew do both their share and his share of the work. One assumption led to another, and ultimately to my conclusion that Ed was a lazy person not doing his job. To this I added my personal belief that everyone needed to work. We had no room for slackers.

At this point I was prepared to confront and, if necessary, punish lazy old Ed. I was ready to take action on my assumptions. This was how what I had observed translated itself almost into the wrong action based on assumptions. The reason I say almost is that I managed to have the presence of mind to ask the job foreman first. It seems Ed wasn't getting a suntan at all. Instead, he was resting because he had developed heat exhaustion from the work he had been doing. If I had acted on assumptions and not learned the facts, I would have acted foolishly, causing unnecessary harm to myself and others.

My story has a point. Yes, it is true that Owen may have diverted the crew and slipped back into the Mike Kane style of manage-ment. But it also could be true that he may not have done so. All you have now are some assumptions from observed infor-mation. I suggest you get some facts before you act. Owen may not be working on his suntan at all.

Let me know how you make out.

TAN made a terrific point. In response, I was determined not to act on my assumptions. I realized that if I did, I could be making a huge mistake and might alienate someone who was trying to do a good job. In a much calmer state of mind, I arose and headed off to find Owen. I found him exactly where I expected, super-vising the work on Line #2.

"Owen, can I talk with you a minute?"

"Sure Todd what can I do for you? By the way, the job here is going really well. I know we'll be done by next Friday."

"Owen, this isn't about Line #2. This morning I saw Jonah and Jacob at Line #3. I thought they were dedicat-ed to the Line #2 project. What's up?" I said this in a neu-tral, non-accusatory tone. I didn't want Owen to think I was blaming him for anything. At least not yet.

"Todd, I know I promised you that I wouldn't divert the crew and I have not done so since we talked. I believe in what you, Pat, and the rest of the steering team are doing. I would not undermine it in any way, shape, or form. In fact, running the Line #1 conversion and now the Line #2 project is one of the high points of my career. Nevertheless, I did move Jonah and Jacob this morning."

"Why?" I asked.

"Under Mike's rule, the mechanics didn't rotate among the lines. All they knew were the lines where they were assigned. And while the lines are pretty much the same, Line #3 has several quirks. Only the guys who worked there really understood how to fix them.

"This morning I got a real emergency call from Line #3. They needed help or they were going to shut down. I know I promised you not to move anyone, but Jonah and Jacob are the only ones who could help. I did what I believed you would want me to do. The choice I had was to comply rigidly with the directive, like when I worked for Mike, or use my head and save production. I can assure you that when the work was done, they returned to Line #2. The good news is that Line #3 didn't miss a beat and the problem was corrected."

All I could think of was that TAN had been right once again. I had almost acted incorrectly based on erroneous assumptions. I had just experienced a major life-changing event and promised myself that, in the future, I would always get the facts first. For me, decisions made based on assumptions were a thing of the past. All I could do with Owen was shake his hand and say, "keep up the good work" as I turned to leave.

THE WEB OF CHANGE
AND C-RCFA

The balance of the week and a good bit of the next flew by. Line #1 was producing Epsilon as planned and the Line #2 conversion project was nearing completion. The Line Down PM process seemed to be working well. Every time the Epsilon line was down for a feed or packaging change, planned PM work was conducted. Lines #3 and #4 were also running well. The correction of the belt problem seemed to have cleared up a major issue for both lines. Nevertheless, I had been approached by operations supervisors from these lines asking when we could implement the Line Down PM program for them.

Everyone seemed reasonably satisfied that what we had described as our game plan at the two town meetings was coming to pass. People were able to form this opinion because they had information about what was going on in the plant. This information had been provided courtesy of *The Tractium Times*, our weekly newsletter, published by Lois and Dani. They had input not only from the steering team but also from many other employees throughout the plant who were involved with all of the changes taking place. At times it seemed that *The Tractium Times* had more information about what was going on than I did!

Another item of interest is that everyone knew when the visit was to occur. If they forgot how many days remained, *The Tractium Times* reminded them weekly by publishing the number right below the banner. In addition, a countdown chart was posted at the entrance to the plant and updated daily so that no one would forget. I was never certain who put it there or who updated it, but it certainly made its point. Time was getting short.

We were all feeling pretty good. It seemed to me that over the previous two months we had individually and collectively passed through the Valley of Despair. We were moving forward. The real problem seemed to be with me. I didn't feel comfortable. I guess I was feeling the let down from the few months since Mike's death. On the surface, it would have appeared that we had essentially changed our world. Still, I couldn't avoid the feeling that more was required.

I had e-mailed TAN right after my recognition that Owen really didn't divert the crew to Line #3 on an arbitrary request from operations. Owen had analyzed the problem and made the correct, fact–based decision. On the other hand, I was embarrassed by what I had almost done. Fortunately I had the presence of mind to contact TAN and had learned about the difference between assumptions and facts first. Nevertheless, I was embarrassed.

I sent TAN several other e-mails regarding our work status and how we had re-worked the goal achievement model using his spiral-learning technique. All of these had received a positive response for which I was grateful. After all, even though I didn't know TAN, he was my mentor and his acknowledgment that we were on the right track was immensely encouraging.

But today was different. I couldn't explain how I felt. It was almost like I knew something was missing, but didn't know how to identify it, much less correct it. There was a gap that needed to be filled. That was what I described in my most recent e-mail to TAN. As always I got my reply rather quickly.

 To: Todd Bradley
From: TAN

Todd, what you described is not uncommon. Bringing change to an organization is difficult, especially an organization as dysfunctional as the one run by Mike. What makes change so dif-

ficult is that it is multifac-
eted. As you have learned, you
need to take into consideration
the eight elements of change
(leadership, work process,
structure, group learning, technology, communications, interrelationships, and rewards) and
the four elements of culture
(organizational values, role
models, rites and rituals, and
the cultural infrastructure) —
and not only individually, but
also collectively. That is a
hard thing to do!

I'd like to introduce you to a
survey that might give you some
of the answers you seek, and
help you navigate your way.
First, however, I need you to
understand that you are not
going to get statistically accurate information from this survey. It will provide you with
subjective information that
will, in turn, allow you to
focus corrective action in the
right areas.

The survey is called the Web of
Change. The reason for the name
is because the radar diagram
that summarizes the survey
results looks like a spider web.
The eight elements of change are

the eight radial axes. Each element has five questions which
are scored based on whether
those taking this survey strongly disagree (0 points), disagree
(1 point), are neutral (2
points), agree (3 points) or
strongly agree (4 points) with
the statement. Based on this
structure, the maximum score for
any element can be 20 at the
high-end or 0 at the low end. By
completing the entire survey,
you get a representation of your
areas of strength and those
areas where improvement may be
needed.

The result of a typical web of
change survey might look like
the following:

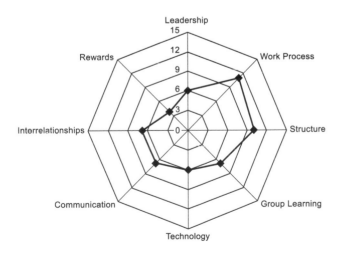

The scores for each element on the web can be viewed as 0-4 very poor, 5-8 poor, 8-12 average, 12-16 good, and 16-20 very good. As you can see in this sample web, work process and structure are good; leadership, group learning, technology communications and interrelationships are average; and rewards is in the poor range. Elements that score poor and very poor are the areas where work is needed.

Todd, applying the web of change survey may help you fill that gap that you have. I am attaching the survey file to this e-mail so that you can use it to identify your strengths and areas for improvement. Contact me when you are done and wc'll discuss the next step, which is your corrective action.

(Note to those reading this story. I have included the web of change survey (hard copy) at the end of the book if you would like to try it for your company. Todd Bradley)

I opened the file and reviewed the questions. I also practiced with the survey by entering different scores to see what the web of change looked like. I loved the idea.

Here was a way to take intangible elements (the eight elements of change) and create a chart showing us how we were doing. Furthermore, if we were willing to accept the information as subjective, we could easily identify areas of needed improvement. This was just what I had been searching for to address my concern that something was missing. I couldn't wait to get the steering team involved and see what the results would be. Our next meeting was Monday so I would have to wait through the weekend.

On Monday the steering team meeting began with very good news. Owen reported that the modifications to Line #2 were completed on schedule. Line #2 was now capable of producing all tractium products, including Epsilon if required to meet product demand. Owen also reported that the Line Down PM program was in place. Crews, parts, and detailed plans were ready to be implemented for all short-duration outages.

Lois reported that she, Dani, and Owen — who all had contacts at the other sites — were gathering line production and reliability data so we could see where we stood versus the other sites: our sister plants. I commented that we were getting into our longer-term initiatives, but Lois responded, "Todd, all we are doing is gathering information. What harm can that do?" I had to agree.

The next item on the agenda was mine. It read "The Web of Change." The term certainly got the group's attention because it was one with which they were not familiar. I was glad that during the weekend I had thoroughly reviewed the material TAN had sent; I was much better prepared to explain it to the group. I started by describing my sense over the previous few weeks that something was missing, and how I could not put my finger on it. Then I discovered a survey that, with some modification, might give us insight into whether or not we had missed anything. I wanted to credit TAN. But who would have believed that for the last couple of months our efforts had been guided through a series of e-mails from an unknown, unnamed person? They would have thought I was crazy. And they may have been right!

It took some explaining, but the Web of Change concept was ultimately not difficult at all. After a few examples which I had previously prepared, they understood the concept. The real problem was that they were so energized with our success to date that many were unwilling to admit that there still could be areas for improvement. Our discussions about continuous improvement were lost in their collective elation over the change they had introduced to the plant.

Pete Jackson, one of the quieter members of the team, broke the impasse. "You know, I have been feeling the same thing as Todd although I couldn't put my finger on the problem. Maybe we should each complete the Web of Change survey separately. Then we can look at both our own scores and the average score of the group for each element. We could see if there were any issues we still needed to address. After all, it wouldn't take that long to try it!"

It still took some convincing. In the end, however, everyone agreed to take the survey. Each of us would answer the 40 questions and we would develop an individual web of change diagram of the average score for each of the elements. I volunteered to gather the data and create a web of change diagram. The team agreed to spend the rest of the day answering the questions and getting their responses back to me. We would reconvene Wednesday to discuss the results.

During the next day, everyone completed the survey and turned in their scores. From their input I created a table with all of their scores. I didn't include names. I just numbered the inputs from one through eight to represent each of the members of the steering team. That way there was no issue or questions to be asked if one person's scores were vastly different from someone else's. Also on this table I averaged the scores for each question. I haven't included all the specific scores. The output is what is really important.

Having all of this information allowed me to create a web of change diagram. I included a high–low score chart so that the team could see the range of scores around each average. This wasn't one of the charts I had originally planned to develop. I realized that it might help us focus our discussion on the low scoring elements with wide variations in individual scores. The web and high–low diagrams are both shown on page 227.

When we reassembled on Wednesday, I handed out the charts. It wasn't surprising to any of the team members that we had rated ourselves as "good" in six of the eight elements, very good in leadership, and poor on rewards. Even the poor score was to have been expected. Under Allen, ATPCo wasn't very good in the area of rewarding performance.

The question on everyone's mind was the point of this exercise if it only validated what we already knew. We had done well and the chart showed it. We did examine the high–low chart as well, but the numbers were not very revealing. The group learning, technology, and reward elements all had low scores when compared to

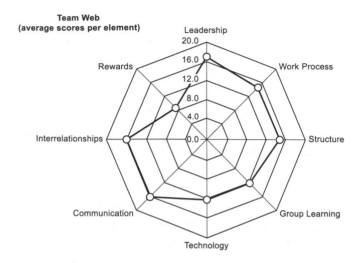

the rest, but we were able to explain those issues as well. To the team, the exercise seemed a waste of time.

Then Gene raised a question that made all of us stop in our tracks. "Let me ask all of you a question. It may help us get a better fix on whatever problem Todd thinks exists. It seems obvious to me, and it should be equally obvious to all of you, that we feel good about what we have accomplished. So why wouldn't we rate

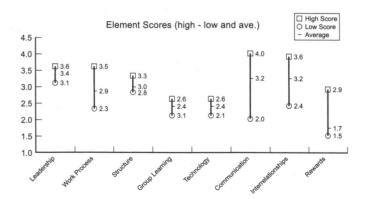

ourselves well? It only makes sense. But our goal, the one about people, is not to deliver the new ATPCo for us. It is to deliver the change for everyone. So what I propose is that my union stewards and I let the workforce take the survey. Then we can compare it to our results from today and see if the workforce thinks we are as good as we think we are. If nothing else, it will be a reality check for us. Maybe it will identify areas for improvement."

Several members of the steering team were immediately in favor of the idea while others took some convincing. I'm not sure why. Maybe they thought the workforce would think all that we had done was just for show and a waste of time. What finally convinced everyone was the simple fact that, like it or not, we needed to know how the workforce viewed our efforts. Gene indicated he could get a good representation of the workforce surveyed by Friday afternoon. We all agreed to proceed and targeted 80% of the plant population as what we would consider a good sample. Once again I agreed to summarize the data and have it ready for our next weekly steering team meeting.

To improve communications, Lois and Dani issued a special edition of The Tractium Times explaining the reason for the survey. They also noted that we would share the results with everyone. They did such a great job of distributing the special edition throughout the plant that by Thursday everyone was informed. By Friday afternoon, Gene and his union stewards distributed an enormous stack of surveys on my desk. Over 90% of the plant's employees had participated!

It took a good bit of the weekend to log all the input and then create the composite web of change dia-

Two Way

	Max	Team	Workforce	Delta
Leadership	20	17.1	11.1	6.0
Work Process	20	14.3	9.9	4.4
Structure	20	14.9	10.9	4.0
Group Learning	20	11.9	9.3	2.6
Technology	20	12.0	9.0	3.0
Communication	20	16.1	12.3	3.9
Interrelationships	20	15.9	11.1	4.8
Rewards	20	8.6	6.5	2.1

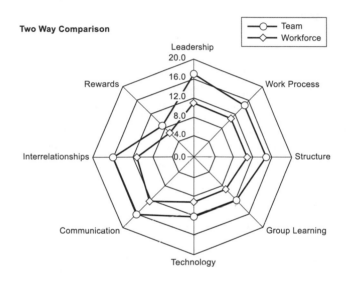

gram showing the steering team's scores and those of the workforce. I have provided the table and the Web diagram for review. These are the same ones I handed out to the team Monday morning. The table shows both sets of scores as well as the differences between them. I labeled these charts the two-way comparison.

The only item on our agenda was the survey review. We observed that the workforce scored the elements similarly to the steering team, but just not as high. That comparison at least told us that we all had similar opinions about what we had accomplished. It also suggested where our strengths and areas for improvement existed. In a way, the workforce survey helped sober us up. We were good — just not as good as we thought we were.

We then discussed the next steps to take. After all, we had some information about where we could improve, yet none of us knew exactly what to do next. That included me because TAN hadn't covered that ground yet. This uncertainty led to a very protracted silence. Everyone was waiting for me to tell them the next steps. Once again, Gene saved the day.

"I have a surprise for all of you," he said. "I expected the results to come in the way they did. I have a lot more contact with the workforce than you do and know what they are thinking and feeling. The truth is: it's my job and I'm good at it. Now I know we are going to work on closing the gaps. Still, I was curious about how the organization felt about where we are now versus where we had been when Mike ran the show. So I ran a second survey of my own.

"Todd, the stewards and I actually conducted two surveys. We conducted yours and the same one with a different question. We asked the workforce to answer the survey as if Mike still ran the plant. While you were making your charts, I made some of my own. Therefore, in addition to the steering team's web, I included the workforce's data which we collected under Pat's leadership and under Mike's leadership. Let's call this the three-way comparison. If any of you have ever wondered if your efforts have made any impact, look at this chart."

Gene distributed his handout. The team then reviewed the workforce's scores rating our performance vs. the scores that they assigned to the plant under

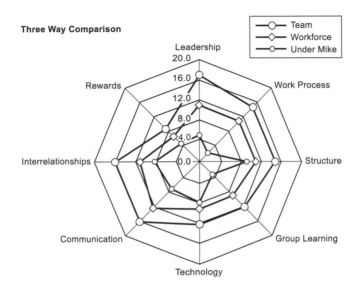

Three Way Comparison

Mike's leadership. The differences were impressive. Pat jumped up and said, "Gene, thanks! This is terrific. You really have done us a great service. In a way, you have validated all the hard work we have done so far. Thank you from the bottom of my heart. This is really good stuff."

Gene was all smiles, but Pat wasn't finished. "Todd, we have made remarkable strides. But there is still a gap between how good we think we are and how the workforce sees our performance. We need to do something about this so we can bring everyone's opinions about our work into alignment. Any ideas?"

I didn't have the answer. Fortunately, I was saved by the bell, in this case, the lunch bell. I hoped that TAN would have an idea and could help me while the team broke for lunch. While they went to the cafeteria, I went

Element	Steering Team Score	Workforce Score	Delta
Leadership	17.1	11.1	6.0
Interrelationships	15.9	11.1	4.8
Work Process	14.3	9.9	4.4
Structure	14.9	10.9	4.0
Communication	16.1	12.3	3.9
Technology	12.0	9.0	3.0
Group Learning	11.9	9.3	2.7
Rewards	8.6	6.5	2.1

to my office in search of TAN and an answer. In my e-mail, I explained my situation. I even sent copies of the various webs and accompanying data. The end of the lunch hour was now fast approaching and I had not yet received a reply. It looked like I was going to have to handle this one by myself.

On my way back to the conference room, I passed a group of mechanics and operators from Line #4 in a heated discussion with Nick and Dani. It seems that one of their main pumps had failed earlier in the shift. Because it was a main pump, we had a spare which was running just fine. Consequently I had not received a call on my radio because there was no line interruption. Everything was okay for now.

The discussion was about the repair process. Both the operators and the mechanics just wanted the pump fixed and back in service as quickly as possible. I understood their feelings, but that was our old way of working. Our new process called for an evaluation so that whatever repair was made would address the root cause of the problem. Then the problem wouldn't re-occur. Dani and Nick were trying to explain as best they could the concept of root cause failure analysis. I listened for a while not wanting to interfere. However, I did inject a few ideas to support their position.

We were late for the steering team meeting so

everyone agreed to pick up the conversation in a few hours. At least everyone was willing to talk and determine a good solution. After all, no one wanted to deal with equipment failure in an unplanned manner. The repair effort resulting from unplanned equipment failure takes a lot of extra work and can be dangerous. Furthermore, we lose money when we can't produce due to unreliable equipment.

As we walked over to the conference room, I had a flash of brilliance. Somewhere in the mysterious recesses of my brain a connection of two seemingly unrelated experiences was made. Thus I figured out a solution to the steering team's dilemma of what we were going to do with the web of change data. Remembering what we had done with Line #3's belt problem, I realized that if we could do root cause failure analysis on our equipment, why couldn't we do "change" root cause failure analysis on low scoring elements within the eight elements of change. This was a novel idea that, when explained, was immediately accepted. I'm not really sure if everyone felt it was a brilliant idea or if they grabbed on to it because they had no other ideas of their own.

We decided to admit that our own scores were somewhat biased. Furthermore, the collective scores of the workforce were how they perceived the Eastern Plant in terms of the eight elements of change. That said, the real areas for improvement were where there were significant differences in the scores of the two groups. We looked at the deltas and summarized them in a table ranking them from the highest delta to the lowest.

As we reviewed our table, it was obvious that the greatest gap between our team and the workforce's survey was leadership. This finding confused everyone when we considered all of our accomplishments achieved over a very short time. Maybe our score was higher than it should have been. Nevertheless, it was our collective score and we decided not to second-guess ourselves. Whatever the reason for the current difference, we scored a great deal better then the workforce's evaluation of leadership under Mike.

In order to get a better understanding of the issues associated with the score, we decided to look at each of the leadership questions and see what the differences were. Maybe a specific component would stand out, giving us a firm starting point for the "change" root cause failure analysis exercise.

Looking at the scores for the individual questions painted a clearer but as yet undefined picture. We agreed

#	Question	Steering Team	Workforce	Delta
1	Rate the reaction of the site personnel to the plant leadership.	3.6	3	0.6
2	The leadership is focused on leading the organization towards a vision of the future.	3.5	2	1.5
3	Management allows the organization freedom to act within a set of predefined boundaries without micromanaging of its efforts.	3.3	2	1.3
4	When the organization develops and implements goals, initiatives and activities, those involved are held accountable for success.	3.1	2	1.1
5	The leader's (at all levels) words about improving are "clearly" supported by their actions.	3.6	2.1	1.5

with all of the statements about leadership. However, as we reviewed the survey results, the workforce was still not convinced. The rest of the team and I thought that a detailed "change" root cause failure analysis would help.

At this point Gene chimed in, "How are we going to do a 'change root cause failure analysis' without insight from the workforce?"

"Gene," I replied. "We need to do an exhaustive analysis and I agree with you about getting input along the way. Didn't you say your union stewards distributed this survey?"

"Yes, they did."

"If that was the case, then they needed to explain what was required as they distributed the survey. I hope that during the process they got other input from the workforce in addition to the answers to the questions. Furthermore, when they are not acting as stewards, they are part of the very group from which we need more insight."

"I have an idea," said Pat. "There are only three stewards. Let's invite them into the group to be part of our discussion and analysis. They already understand the survey so they can quickly learn what we are trying to do. Gene can explain the root cause failure analysis process. Then we can hit the ground running first thing tomorrow."

"Dani and Nick can help as well," I said remembering the discussion in which they were involved before our meeting.

With that settled we adjourned, agreeing to meet the next day. The next morning the small conference room was rather crowded. In attendance were the eight steering team members as well as the three union stewards. Gene, Dani, and Nick had met with them over breakfast and Nick assured me that they understood the process we were going to follow. His assurance convinced me that we could launch right into our change root cause failure analysis discussion. I had never done one of these for a change initiative but had been involved in many equipment failure analyses, the most recent being the Line #3 belt failure. From what I knew of the equipment-related root cause failure analysis efforts, this process was going to take a great deal of time and effort.

The process we were going to follow was the same as any other root cause failure analysis except this one was focused on an intangible element. In this case, the focus was on leadership, not the failure of a tangible piece of equipment. Analyzing failure in leadership could deal only with subjective information with very little factual backup, whereas in the latter case, equipment failure, the focus was quite the opposite. Nevertheless, subjective data — in this case, how the workforce felt about our leadership skills — was a perception of the workforce. As many will tell you, perception is reality.

We began our effort with a definition of the problem. The problem needed to be framed as a question so that we could continually ask "why" in our attempt to reach the root cause. From our knowledge of root cause failure analysis (as limited as it was), we all recognized that if we resolved the root of the problem, we would also resolve the outward manifestations of that problem, in this case, the workforce's feeling of neutrality about the current leadership team.

To help you follow our process, I will provide diagrams and label the parts of the why tree we built. The primary question, "Why does the workforce feel neutral about our leadership?" will be labeled L-0 for level 0. The subsequent levels will be labeled with an "L" and the number of the level as we work our way through the process. I will also assign letters to each of the major items of discussion for reference. Sound complicated? It really isn't, as you will see.

Note to readers:
The full diagram is shown in Appendix 2.

The problem we were trying to solve had been clearly identified. Why does the workforce feel neutral about our leadership skills during the time since Pat took over after Mike's death?

The next part, which I believe was the most difficult, was listing the major reasons why we thought the workforce was neutral. The stewards, Nick, Dani, and Gene had a far better sense of why. They listed many reasons, all of which I wrote on our flipchart. The management side of the team played the "devil's advocate" role and helped the entire team to test the validity of the statements. In the end, we arrived at five reasons we felt the workforce was neutral. These are listed as L-1 (for level 1) and have the following letters assigned to differentiate them from one another.

A. The leadership team hasn't been in place for long and they are skeptical of the final outcome.

B. A few short-term changes do not undo years of mismanagement.

C. Lack of trust is based on past experience.

D. We see a lot of talk but not a lot of action.

E. They are scared.

Typically at this point in the root cause failure analysis process you assign scores to each of the level 1 items. A score of five would indicate that we thought the reason was "highly likely", a score of three "likely," and a score of one "unlikely." Based on these scores, we would then concentrate our efforts on the items that received a score of five. However, this approach is not exactly the one we followed. Yes, we discussed and assigned scores. But we decided to ask why for all of the different reasons to see what we could flush out.

Although Items A, B, and D scored only one point each, we still went through the exercise of asking "why." Item D had only one level and we were unable to create any levels of greater depth. Our inability to develop this one to a greater depth was frustrating. With some discussion, we recognized the reasons. D was just frustration with the time it had taken to get the changes in place following Mike's death. We dismissed this item because 1) it really hadn't been that long, and 2) the people making the comments didn't fully understand the difficulties. One positive outcome was our agreement as a team to use *The Tractium Times* to better communicate all of the changes that were underway, thereby helping us manage people's expectations.

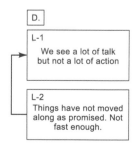

Items A and B were also developed only one level deep. The reason these were scored was that the workforce was projecting on to our team their past experience with management, Mike, and probably others. Although we all seemed to think this bias was unfair, we clearly understood how they felt. We agreed that if we had been in their position, we probably would feel the same way. By asking "why" repeatedly, we did not get any insight to our current leadership problems. Instead, we only saw the problems of the past managers.

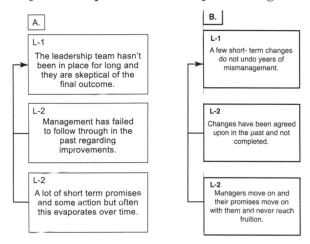

Item C — Lack of trust based on past experience — scored higher, a three. Although it still focused on past experience, we were able to drill down three levels to a statement that did apply to our team. The workforce believed that, with little experience, Pat would revert to the old way of doing things; the former ATPCo culture. The stewards clarified that this concern was about a possible return to the ways and behaviors of Mike Kane. Pat denied any possibility that this could happen. Still, I clearly remembered his actions during the controversial

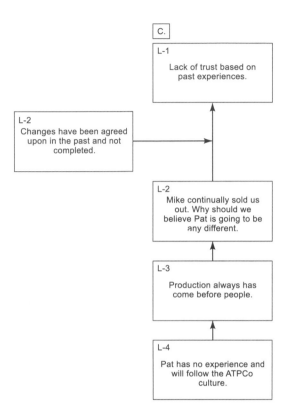

teleconference with Allen and wasn't entirely sure. I did allow the team to get a chance to discuss the matter. However, we had no real proof that reversion would happen and ultimately we moved on.

Item E — They're scared — was an entirely different story. As soon as we started discussing this item, we knew it would receive a score of five. We explored three "why" chains. Subsequently, we dismissed the one about the visit because it was purely speculation. The other two were not; they were real. As we drilled down to the lowest level in each, the root of the workforce's neutral

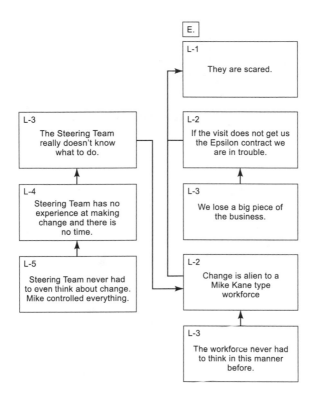

scores became apparent.

The employees were scared on two levels. First they had no experience with change. In fact, they had no experience even thinking for themselves. When you live in a world that is defined by "my way or the highway," how could you be expected to even consider thinking for yourself if you wanted to stay employed? Second, they had no faith that we had any more experience at managing change than they did. Item C was hinting at this, but item E brought the message home loud and clear. We had found the root. What we were not sure of was what to do about it.

Everyone looked at me, I guess in the hope that I had a magic pill or a quick fix to the problem. I didn't. However, I did have a few ideas. "Folks, the solution to this issue is not easy. The problem is one of lack of confidence in us and, from the workforce's perspective, in themselves as well. I think that our actions over the next several weeks should address these concerns. These actions include finalizing our plan to win the Epsilon contract, actually winning it, and planning for what we will do after we win it. We can show them that we are walking the talk of the new ATP3Co. We just need the time.

For the workforce, they need more than time. They need personal evidence and direct experience to show them that they all have the ability to make a difference, not only for the company but also for their own future. Our goal achievement model addresses some of this in our People goal, but not enough. We need step change — a major way that redefines how we work and how the workforce is part of that work.

We need to redo our three People initiatives. We don't need just to communicate on a more frequent basis. We need a communications strategy where everyone knows all the time the work that is being undertaken to promote successful change. We don't need just to add a few more members to the steering team and have it continue to be essentially run by the senior plant management group. As senior managers we need to turn the steering team over to a joint team of middle managers and the workforce representatives to help run the plant. Last, we don't just need to have teams working on the lines. We need self-directed work teams that run the lines."

I was out of breath but went on, "We don't need a new ATP3Co. At this point, we need a redefined ATP3Co. But, I am not advocating this now. After all, we need the contract first. However, after we get the contract, we need to rework our goal achievement model again and present our strategy to upper management. If we get the contract with what we have done so far, just imagine what we can achieve with even a few of the ideas I just laid out."

I stopped and looked at the other members. For a moment everyone was silent. Then everyone began to speak at once. They were excited about results and the prospect for their collective future. We had completed our "change" root cause failure analysis, but accomplished even more. The web of change and the "change" root cause failure analysis exercise had been the catalyst.

Meanwhile, our last hurdle — the site visit by our potential customer — was just two weeks away.

CHAPTER 14

THE VISIT

The final two weeks prior to our potential customer's visit flew by. The steering team spent their time preparing in great detail. We needed a well-developed, detailed presentation that would show our potential customer what we could do for them. We had accomplished a lot, but it was all for naught if we didn't show the customer that we were a reliable operation; one that they would want for a long term supplier. We spent hours in meetings developing the agenda. More important, we were developing the substance needed to support the agenda.

The presentation was going to focus on a straightforward agenda and a detailed PowerPoint slide deck. Using PowerPoint in this manner would allow us to structure our presentation. We made certain that every point we wanted to make was properly delivered. With this task almost finished — I say almost because we kept changing the slides to make them better — we moved on to determine who was going to present the material.

We all agreed that Pat would start the discussion and review the agenda. By unanimous decision, I was tagged to make the presentation. There are two reasons that everyone thought I should be the spokesperson. First, no one else in the group wanted the job! Second, the others believed I could best present the concepts we developed to improve our plant's performance and explain how we put them into practice.

I was honored to be chosen, but I definitely was not going to let the rest of the team off the hook so easily. Several parts of the presentation, such as the union relationship and their role in the maintenance process, were to be presented by Gene and Nick because they had a deeper involvement than I had in this phase of the business. Furthermore, having them make the presentation would add another level to the credibility of the message. We worked extremely hard on this presentation. By the Tuesday a week prior to the visit we were ready. All that remained were the dry runs we had planned to practice our delivery.

By the way, I did get an e-mail back from TAN about how to work with our web of change results. By the time I got it, however, we had already done the analysis that I have previously described and recognized that we needed to do more with our People goal. This was especially true if we were going to reduce the level of workforce fear, engage them in our change effort, and ultimately succeed.

The interesting thing about TAN's response is that he suggested we average the two scores — the steering team's score and the workforce's score — and perform the analysis on the lowest scoring element. In this case, the lowest scoring element would have been rewards. Had we used TAN's approach, we undoubtedly would have identified valuable actions that would increase the employees' feelings of value. Yet I really believe that what we did with our analysis was even better and achieved more immediate benefit.

Believe it or not, TAN agreed once I had explained our process and its outcome. His response was very interesting. It was short and said simply, "as one learns, at times the teacher becomes the student." I guess we had taught him something that he could use in his own work (whatever that was).

It was also at around this time I got another message from Allie. She had narrowed down TAN's location further to a small town at the California-Arizona border called Blythe. She promised me that within two weeks she would give me an address, thereby completing her contract. I was happy about her success and the fact that she didn't need any more money to finish it. I wasn't sure how I was going to get across the country so that I could finally meet and talk with TAN. But I knew two things. First I would make the effort. Second it would have to wait until after the prospective customer had visited the plant. Therefore, I put aside any thought of meeting TAN and focused instead on what would be our defining moment, for good or bad.

Meanwhile, the plant was running well. The lines were at maximum. As we had planned, we had switched Line #2 to Epsilon because Line #1 alone was not able to satisfy the demand. Epsilon was a popular product and we couldn't make enough of it. We all were certainly glad we had converted Line #2 so that it could serve multiple purposes. The best part of our progress was that our line down PM program, along with some predictive techniques newly introduced by the engineering department, had made the lines highly reliable.

In fact Pat, Owen, Lois, and others who had contacts throughout the company had acquired data not only about our reliability but also about reliability at the other ATPCo plants. This information was simultaneously revealing and disturbing, and we could never tell anyone where we obtained the information. If we had, the people involved would certainly have lost their jobs.

The analysis didn't take very long. When it was complete, I understood more about ATPCo than I really wanted to know. The reason Allen could not have replaced Pat or me when we had the blow up about Line #1 was that Allen was working closely with several banks to obtain loans to keep the company in business. The other plant managers that he could have sent in as replacements couldn't be spared from their own sites. Each and every one of them was struggling with very serious reliability issues of their own. In fact, when our reliability figures since Mike's death were compared to the charts for the other sites, we weren't simply reliable in comparison; we were the most reliable of all five plants in the ATPCo network. No wonder that the other managers couldn't be spared!

Pat and I wanted to share this information.

Considering how we had obtained it, we decided to keep it our little secret, at least officially. Remember that several of the steering team members were involved in obtaining the information. The rest were told the results. Although sworn to secrecy, we still had at least one of the biggest gossips in the plant on our team. We couldn't distribute the information officially. Nevertheless, I felt certain that at least one element of the cultural infrastructure would see that everyone knew how well we were doing. I was proven correct within one day.

Fortunately we had our agenda and PowerPoint presentation ready the week prior to the visit. As it turns out, Allen wanted to see it and review it with us. As president he certainly had that prerogative. Still, I sincerely hoped that we were not going to have a repeat performance like the last time Allen wanted to interfere. Well, we didn't have a repeat performance. Unfortunately, it was worse. The teleconference started out well as we reviewed our production levels. We then tried without much success to explain what we were doing to improve ourselves across the board. The discussion soon turned to the upcoming visit. We reviewed our agenda and our plan for the presentation, followed by a detailed, slide-by-slide review. Allen had some questions and some suggestions that I thought actually improved upon the work we had done in some areas. I was on edge, however, waiting for some problem to emerge that Pat and I had not expected. It did.

"Gentlemen," Allen said. "You have done an excellent job. When I present this information to our prospective customer, I will make sure that you get all of the credit. I plan to arrive the evening before. We can all have dinner and go over the remaining details. Thank you. I will have my administrative assistant let you know when I will arrive." With that he hung up, never giving us any chance to reply.

I just sat there. I couldn't speak. I couldn't do anything until I got myself somewhat calmed down. I could tell from Pat's facial expression and body language he felt the same. It was as if everything we had done was about to be ruined and we couldn't stop it. From our perspective, Allen had no more idea of what we had actually accomplished or what we planned for the future than the man in the moon. There was no way that he could adequately present the material. Nor was there any way he could show the passion we all felt about our new direction. Without that passion and commitment, we did not believe there was any way Allen could win the contract.

I was so concerned and upset that I had to excuse myself. I returned to my office to think about what had just happened. Although I had promised Pat I would be back, I couldn't promise a solution to our new and most serious dilemma.

Back at the office I couldn't calm myself down. It seemed as if all of the work we had done was about to go up in smoke. With no immediate answer to my problem, I e-mailed TAN. It must have been one of those days that he was sitting at his computer because I got an answer within fifteen minutes.

```
To: Todd Bradley
From: TAN

Your problem is serious and I
have no solution for you. For
this one you don't need me any-
```

```
way. All I can advise are two
things that one of my former
managers told me years ago. The
situation was different, but the
advice was sound for that situa-
tion as well as the one in which
you are currently involved. He
said, "Take charge, but always
do the right thing and do it to
the best of your ability."
That's my advice for you. Let me
know how it all works out.
```

That wasn't what I wanted to hear, but TAN was right. I had to take charge and do the right thing; only I wasn't sure what the right thing was supposed to be. I called Pat and told him that as much as I wished I had an answer, I didn't, and I was going home. During the rest of the week, I appeared as if all was normal, at least by my outward appearance. But inside, I was far from normal. Instead, I was very upset. I wasn't eating well and sleep was, at best, elusive. Even when I did get to sleep I had very disturbing dreams; I'd wake up as tired as I had been before lying down. I shared my problem with Susan and Paws. Unfortunately Susan, as much as she wanted to, couldn't help. As for Paws, if he had a solution, he wasn't talking.

Things continued this way until the day before Allen was due to arrive. It was then that I finally made my decision. I explained it to Susan. As always, she told me that she had complete confidence that whatever I did would be in the best interests of everyone. My problem was that I couldn't tell anyone at work of my plan, including Pat. I told Pat that I couldn't explain anything, but that I was doing what I believed to be in everyone's best interest. I assured him that if he had trust in me, things would work out. As much as he pressed me, I wouldn't reveal my plan of action.

I didn't see Pat the rest of the afternoon. At 4:00 PM we left to meet Allen at his hotel for dinner. We got there early and waited at the bar until the scheduled meeting time of 5:00 PM. Fortunately, the wait was short. I was more nervous than I had ever been in my entire life. On the other hand, Pat seemed resolved to whatever was about to happen.

Promptly at 5:00 PM Allen appeared from the elevator. He actually seemed happy to see us and warmly shook our hands. As it happened, Allen had selected a hotel with a really great restaurant, so we chose not to leave the hotel for dinner. The initial discussion was composed of small talk about families and Allen's famous golf game. I just wanted to get to the point of the meeting but unfortunately you need to go through the pleasantries first. Then we had what probably was an excellent meal. I wouldn't know! I was so nervous and on edge that I could barely eat. Then over coffee Allen addressed the reason we were there; the upcoming visit from the Tractium Distribution Company or TDC as they preferred to be called.

As I had expected, Allen had changed all of the slides and reworked the agenda. He was going to present the same old ATPCo business strategy which, by the way, had absolutely nothing to do with all of the work we had accomplished over the last 90 days. After Allen had explained all of the changes, Pat looked over at me. I knew it was my turn. This was going to be more than a simple discussion. This was about to be a defining moment in my life and that of the Eastern Plant, for better or for worse.

"Allen," I said. "I respect you as a person. You have taken tractium and ATPCo from nothing to a major industry and a major company within the industry. However, I want to point out to you that much has changed at the Eastern Plant since Mike died. We aren't the same plant. I guarantee that we aren't the same people we were 90 days ago. Therefore, it is important that you let the steering team handle the presentation as we planned and as we have laid out for you during our last teleconference. If you do, I will guarantee we will get the contract. I'll stake my job on it."

"Todd, I hear what you are saying but my decision stands. I'll do the presentation and you, Pat, and the steering team of yours can answer any questions that TDC has about the information."

"That isn't going to work. The steering team members have lived with this effort. Not only do they know the material, but they are passionate about the work that they have accomplished. They also have incredibly strong feelings about what they plan to do at the Eastern plant in the future. If you make the presentation, that passion won't come through. Allen, it is vitally important that we show this emotion and our belief in all that we have achieved."

"I'm sorry Todd, but I am the president of this company and I will do the presentation myself. That's my final decision and this discussion is over."

Allen was now very angry. He was about to ask for the check, but I wasn't finished. "Allen, before you leave, I'd like to show you something." On this note, I pulled out the confidential financial records we had obtained.

"Allen, if you don't win this contract and if I read this information correctly, then ATPCo is in serious trouble. It may even be out of business."

Allen was even angrier now, but I didn't let him interrupt. I pressed on. "I also have charts showing plant reliability and production rates for all of the sites since Mike's death. The Eastern Plant isn't just reliable and producing as much product as the other sites. We are vastly better than all of the other plants on all counts. That is why you couldn't send another plant manager to take over for Mike. The other sites are struggling just to keep their plants running.

Finally, if you don't allow me to handle the presentation and the visit, then I won't be at your meeting because I will no longer be working for you. I care about this company, its people, and all that we have accomplished more than you will ever know. And, although you may not believe it, I am doing my best right now to help you avoid a massive mistake."

Allen's face was so red I thought that he was going to have a stroke on the spot. "Todd, you're fired. Don't even bother to show up tomorrow because I personally will make certain you are denied access to the plant."

I sat back in my chair defeated. I had tried my best and laid it all on the line, but to no avail. I looked over at Pat expecting to see him as I had during the previous confrontation with Allen, sinking down in his chair in an attempt to disappear. But that was not what I saw. In fact, he was sitting upright and leaning forward with a hard look on his face. "Allen," he said. "If you fire Todd, then I quit as well. Do the presentation yourself. I'm going to go and find a job with a good company that will still be around in six months."

"Fine, then you're fired too. I don't need the two of you. I'll get this done with the rest of the steering team and hire new managers to replace you. I need people who are on my team, not people who undermine my efforts."

"No you won't," said Gene. I was shocked. Where did Gene come from? I looked up and there was Gene along with the rest of the steering team. What were they doing here? I didn't get a chance to ask because Gene had more to say. "Allen, if you persist, we all quit. And one more thing, just so you know we are serious. If we quit, then the union membership which I represent will all walk off the job at exactly 9:00AM tomorrow morning. Todd and Pat have worked wonders at the plant and with the people. I once told Todd that if he worked on our behalf I would support him. He never let us down and I in turn will not let him down now. Everyone at the plant is behind our team 100%. So now let's talk about how the meeting tomorrow is really going to happen."

Now it was Allen's turn to sink down in his chair. I don't think he had ever experienced anything like this in his entire career. After all, he had a Mike Kane work ethic. Loyalty of this sort was unheard of in his world. He knew that his plan for the meeting was defeated, but I needed to help him save face. After all, he still was the president of the firm. I wasn't trying to defeat the man; I was trying to save the company.

"Alright, everyone, let's take a step back and figure this all out to everyone's satisfaction," I said. "First let's adjourn to the lobby. We're blocking the waitresses and disturbing the customers." Allen paid the check and we all filed out to the hotel lobby. Once there we regrouped and I laid out my plan. Before this meeting I had developed a game plan hoping against hope that I could convince Allen to let us handle the visit. I had never expected what had just happened. Still, the plan I had put together could still work.

The folded agenda that I pulled out of my pocket had Allen kicking off the meeting and then quickly turning it over to Pat. Allen would save face but we would control the meeting and present the material as we had developed it. To insure that we stayed with the plan, I had prepared a second document for Allen. It contained a set of talking points he could use. Many of them praised the team's work; others assured the customer that he and the corporation were behind us 100%. Allen had no real choice but to agree. He grabbed the agenda and talking points from my hand and coldly said, "I'll see all of you in the morning." He then turned his back on us and walked to the elevator.

After he was gone I just stood there. I couldn't move. Nevertheless, I needed to know how the steering team conspiracy had been orchestrated. "Pat," I said. "How did you and everyone else know about my plan? I purposely didn't tell any of you because I didn't want you to get involved with something that could have cost you your jobs. That's why I planned to go this alone."

"We couldn't allow that," Pat responded. "After all, you have constantly told us that we are a team. A team puts the needs of the group ahead of their own individual needs."

"But there was no way you could have known." At least I thought so until I saw Susan walk out of the bar.

At exactly 9:00 AM the next morning Allen, Pat, the steering team, and I introduced ourselves to the team from the Tractium Distribution Company or TDC.

Three executives attended for TDC: Shane Franks, the president; John Parker, the chief financial officer; and Paul Gamble, the manager of TDC's plant operations. As planned, Allen opened the meeting, welcomed our visitors, and explained what we had planned for their visit. He also introduced all of us on the steering team. He was so upbeat and polished that no one would ever have known what had transpired the previous evening. He even followed the bulleted script that I had given him and didn't deviate, not even once.

Next up was Pat who explained at a high level all that we had done since he took over after Mike's death. He worked from the slide presentation and used charts showing the reliability of the lines and our production rates to back up his words. When he was finished, Gene took over. He explained the role of the workforce from the membership on the steering team all the way down to the role of the people working on the line.

Then it was my turn. My explanation centered on the vision and the goal achievement model, both how we had developed it and how it had been revised for the future. I also added information about the Line Down PM program and the newly-emerging predictive maintenance program. Last but not least I described the web of change process, the survey, and how we used it to enhance the goal achievement model. My presentation took over three hours because the TDC executives had a great many questions, all of which we answered to the best of our ability. In fact, I even promised to send them the file with the web survey so that they could complete it at their sites. All through my presentation I kept looking over at Allen sitting in the back of the room, but I could not get a read from his facial expression or body language.

After lunch we went on a plant tour and explained every detail of our operation. Again our visitors had a great many questions. They even stopped and asked questions of workers on the line. After the TDC executives moved on, many of the workers gave me the three-fingers up sign and grinned. By the time we finished the tour it was 2:30. Pat wrapped up the discussion with any last-minute questions back at the conference room.

It was then Shane Franks's turn. He thanked us both for our time and for the openness and honesty of the presentation and answers to their questions. He seemed pleased and told us that he was very impressed with our operation.

As he finished, Allen asked, "Well Shane what's the next step? I am sure you want to review today's presentation back at your office and determine your direction. I would like to suggest that we meet again in a few weeks. My administrative assistant can coordinate the details with you, but of course that's your call."

"Actually," Shane said, "we would like some time for ourselves right now. If you would excuse us, we would like to use your conference room for a short while. We will give you a call when we are finished."

We adjourned to the hall expecting that their discussion would not to take very long. We clearly did not know what the TDC executives were doing. Each minute seemed like an hour. As time went on, Allen became increasingly agitated. I knew that if we didn't get the contract my career with ATPCo was over. Based on my track history with Doug, Mike, and now Allen, it probably was over even if we did get the contract. At the moment, those considerations did not bother me. I was much more worried about everyone else. It wasn't encouraging to me that the TDC team believed that they could make a decision of this enormity before they left the plant, but the die was cast.

After about forty-five minutes, Paul Gamble came out and asked us to return. We slowly filed in to the conference room not knowing what to expect, yet recognizing we were about to learn our fate. John Parker stood up and said, "Your team has truly worked wonders here. I know for a fact that this plant was in shambles while it was being run by Mike. You might wonder how I know this. Ralph Johnston —your former Eastern Plant finance manager — told me so. He was one of the very bright people Mike fired for no reason other than he wouldn't comply with Mike's atrocious management style. Why would he tell me this? Well, Ralph happens to be my son-in-law. He is currently a very successful and highly regarded member of the TDC management team. He told me what I should expect today and I am happy to say he was very wrong. Allen, you have empowered these people to do things in a very short time that are nothing short of astounding. We are all extremely pleased with everything we have seen."

"So John, what's the bottom line? Do we have the contract?" Allen asked.

"Well, Allen, I am sorry to say we can't give you a contract to provide Epsilon as one of our suppliers."

I watched Allen turn an incredible shade of white, but John wasn't finished.

"Allen, what we would like to do is something far different. We would like you to become the sole supplier of Epsilon for TDC — a partnership, if you will. We would like to build another Epsilon line in your plant. It would be owned by TDC but run by ATPCo. We have talked this over and we all believe that together we can be a major national presence manufacturing Epsilon right here in your Eastern Plant. I know that a great many details will need to be ironed out, but what do you think about the idea? Oh, one other thing. We want Todd to teach us the process that he and the team used to convert this plant and its people from what I know to be one of the worst plants around to one of the best."

Allen's face quickly switched expressions from one of impending doom to one of extreme elation, the same look that was on everyone's face in the room. After agreeing to let the lawyers work out the details, the meeting adjourned.

Anticipating a positive outcome to the meeting, Pat and I had arranged for Lois to order food and beverages, which were now set up in the waiting area. If we had failed to gain the contract, we thought we could always have used the food as a last supper, but now that wasn't necessary. The next hour was spent talking with the TDC representatives in a much more social setting. Everyone enjoyed this relaxed setting.

As it was ending, Allen asked for a moment. He thanked the TDC executives for their show of confidence and assured them that our future joint venture would be immensely profitable for all. He also announced that because of the excellent job he had done, Pat was to be named permanent plant manager.

As for me, he said nothing. I guessed Allen believed that praising in public and punishing in private was how he wanted to handle this one. As we were leaving, Allen pulled me aside and simply said, "Call my administrative assistant first thing Monday. Make arrangements to meet me in the corporate office as soon as possible." That was all he said. I acknowledged his request and turned away knowing that my time with ATPCo was short. After all, how many times do you threaten the president of a company and get away with it?

Monday at work felt like Christmas. Everyone was happy with the results of the meeting with TDC. In fact, it took me over an hour to get past everyone who wanted to shake my hand and thank me for what the steering team and I had done. On my desk was a special edition of *The Tractium Times* with the headline "We Win" printed in large letters across the top. I was happy as well, but I knew that very shortly Allen was going to fire me and my career with ATPCo would be over.

With that in mind, I started to get my work in order so that I wouldn't be leaving any loose ends after I left. I also contacted TAN and told him what had happened. As I closed out the e-mail, I knew that my relationship with TAN was coming to an end. I owed him a great deal and asked (for at least the tenth time) what I could do to thank him. I knew he wouldn't answer that question, but I had to ask one last time. The e-mail that I received back was short and to the point. After reading it I felt like I had just lost a best friend.

```
To: Todd Bradley
From: TAN

Congratulations! I knew you
could do it. Now all you need to
remember is that the agreement
between TDC and ATPCo is only
the beginning. It is just the
completion of one spiral. Now
```

you are ready to define the next
one. Never forget that what you
have done was not a project. It
is a process of continuous
improvement that never ends. You
won't be getting any more e-
mails from me. You don't need me
any more. You know what to do.
And, if there is something you
don't know, I have great confidence that you will figure it
out. Have a good life and always
remember that in everything -
reliability is the key to your
salvation.

As far as TAN was concerned that was it, but I
knew otherwise. Allie had pinned down the exact location of TAN in Blythe, California. Because I was going to
visit Allen, I had every intention of dropping in to see
him. I thought that I owed him an enormous debt and
wanted to thank him in person.

CHAPTER 15

THE END GAME

One week later, I arrived bright and early at ATPCo's corporate headquarters. I had spent my evening in the hotel worrying about this meeting. As always when I am under high stress, I didn't sleep very well. My meeting with Allen was the first one on his agenda; I knew that I had been allocated only one hour. Actually I didn't expect it to take that long for Allen to beat me up verbally for some of my actions, and then fire me. I suspected that he had me travel across the country just so he could get the last word in before he showed me the highway.

Back at the plant, the steering team didn't believe that this was Allen's intent at all. Yes, they thought he might take me to task for some choices I made such as hanging up on him or forcing him to let us make the presentation. Still, he couldn't be so vindictive as to fire me after what we had accomplished, or at least, so the team believed. I can't say I agreed with them simply because I knew that the behaviors of people like Mike and Doug were directly the result of Allen's role model. That is why I was scared. I genuinely liked my co-workers and was excited when I thought about the Eastern Plant's future as they built the new Epsilon unit and went into business with TDC. I had worked hard to help us get there and wanted to be a part of it as we moved forward.

Nevertheless, the steering team believed that Allen had other plans. They thought he would want to discuss in detail our plans for the future and how we had reworked our goal achievement model following the Web of Change and C-RCFA. For this reason, they spent considerable time helping me build a succinct presentation that described our accomplishments in the ninety days before the site visit. The slides were designed so that I could convince Allen that our methods were sound, should be retained and could be successfully replicated across the four remaining plants.

My team was so focused on having my presentation be successful that they made me do several dry runs, with Owen pretending to be Allen. He had prepared and asked pointed question designed to anticipate what Allen might ask. If I didn't provide an answer acceptable to the team, they made me stop. We discussed the best response and then they made me rehearse that answer all over again until I got it right. This process took almost two days. However, when we were finished, I believed I was ready for anything Allen could throw at me. I wished I was as confident of a positive outcome as they were, but I knew in my heart what really was about to happen.

ATPCo's corporate office building was not very large. This visit was my first since being hired and I had forgotten its size — I had expected it to be larger. In retrospect, I realized that Allen maintained a very small staff. He preferred to assign the majority of the staff to the plants and use central staff only for coordinating the five plant network.

The receptionist, who was expecting my arrival, immediately sent me to the third floor where Allen maintained his office. This small area was very conservative in its design. The only pictures on the wall were of the five plants and one group picture of Allen's long time friends and co-workers from the early days of ATPCo. In the picture, I recognized Doug, Mike, and the other three plant managers of the ATPCo network. There was also a large collage on the wall showing the different items produced with tractium. Allen was going to have to upgrade the collage now that we were manufacturing Epsilon.

Without much delay Allen's administrative assistant ushered me into Allen's office where he was waiting. He got up from his desk and we shook hands. I could tell that there was no warmth in Allen's handshake. Other than through Allen's attendance at the recent meeting with TDC, several teleconferences, Mike's funeral, and my initial interviews when I was hired. I had never had much interaction with Allen. Rather than sit back down behind his desk with me in front, he directed me to a small round meeting table, a setting that allowed him much closer contact. As nervous as I was, this did not make me feel any calmer. In fact, he increased my level of concern dramatically.

"Todd, thank you for coming," Allen said. "Over the last 90 days, I can truthfully say that we have not gotten along very well. In fact there were two events, the teleconference and the dinner before the TDC visit, where you actually threatened my position as president of this company. We're going to talk about that in a moment. But first I want you to explain in as much detail and time as you need what you've done over the last 90 days. I also want you to outline your plans for the Eastern plant's future. For that reason I've changed the duration of our meeting from the original hour to all morning. I need to have enough time to understand exactly what you and your team did at the Eastern Plant."

I was surprised. Maybe the steering team had been right all along. Yet even after I explained to Allen all that we had done, I still knew that he was going to punish me for my actions. A personality like Allen's would never allow me the liberties that I had taken in my effort to make the Eastern Plant's bid for the tractium contract a success. However, that was going to be the second part of our discussion. I needed to wait until a proper time and the proper opportunity to defend myself.

For now my task was to explain the Eastern Plant's game plan for the future. That outline included what we had done to prepare everyone at the site to be able to achieve our plan. For the next three hours I explained everything. I discussed how we created a new vision for the plant's future and how we applied team concepts so that everyone would work together with the same purpose in mind. I described the Goal Achievement Model, the Eight Elements of Change, the Four Elements of Culture, and how all of these pieces fit together into a comprehensive reliability program. I also explained the Web of Change and the C–RCFA change process, and finally what actions we took in response to what we had learned.

Surprising to me, the presentation we had developed at the plant was perfect. It generated detailed, challenging questions from Allen, which, thanks to my team, I was well prepared to answer. I made very clear to Allen that the initiative may have been started by Pat and me, but the real credit belonged to the men and women at the plant. Although they had been skeptical at the outset, they ultimately embraced the new ideas and collectively made those ideas work.

One last point I emphasized to Allen was that we were producing tractium cheaper and with more reliable processes than our current competition. As a result, we had a firm control over the eastern market. As Allen knew, this position was firmly established after our meeting with the TDC representative the prior week.

When I was finished, I was exhausted. But I also felt terrific about what our plant had accomplished and how well I had explained those accomplishments to Allen. I made a mental note to thank my team for the days they had spent preparing me; they had done really well. I hoped I would get to thank them in person, assuming that at the least I would be allowed back in the plant to collect my personal belongings after being fired.

Meanwhile, Allen gave me no sense of what he was thinking. I had hoped that he would be happy about the plant's accomplishments. However, happiness, or even satisfaction, was far from the reaction I was reading on his face. If I could characterize what I saw, I would say he was very upset with something. Perhaps he was pleased with the outcome of the Eastern plant's efforts, but was now preparing for the part where he would fire me. This could be the only reason he looked like he did. Memories of my experience with Doug came flooding back and I began to get very nervous about the next part of the meeting. However, there was nothing I could do about it.

Allen cleared his throat and took a long drink of water before he spoke, "Todd I have to apologize humbly to you." Well, this was certainly a strange way to start a conversation about firing someone. "I always believed the same way that Mike did. I believed that if you pushed the equipment and the people hard enough, then you always would be able to meet demand. When I first met you at the conference, I thought that the concepts you presented had merit. That's why I hired you. However, I never took the time to try to understand what they meant and what was required to implement them. I just never got past my arrogance to truly understand the benefits they could deliver. What happened when Epsilon was introduced was a wake-up call — a call that I failed to answer properly.

"Even before that, when you initiated some novel reliability concepts at the Western Plant, Doug and I failed to see any value. Instead we punished you. Doug was hoping that you would resign. I am glad that I made him give you the chance to relocate. Then Mike died. Without us 'old school' tractium managers around, you and your team were able to implement vastly improved work concepts. And now look at the results!

"Todd you saved the day. No, strike that. You saved the company as you well know from looking at the financial information you had in your possession last week. Someday you'll have to tell me how you got hold of it. Meanwhile, Todd, for the way I acted towards you, I humbly apologize. Furthermore, I intend to write a letter of apology to everyone at ATPCo. I almost allowed our company to be destroyed from within. I can assure you that I will never allow that to happen again."

I was dumbstruck. I had come to the corporate office expecting to be fired. Instead, what I had just heard from Allen was nothing short of amazing. Not only did he understand his own failures, but he was willing to take ownership for them. I also got the distinct impression that he understood the actions we needed to improve, that he bought into the concepts — all of them.

"Allen, there is no need to apologize," I said. "I always have believed that everything happens for a reason. I believe that even when the reason may not be apparent at the time. I'm just glad that I was in the right place at the right time to do some good, not only for ATPCo, but also for the loyal men and women who make up your company." With that I shook his hand and got up to leave, thinking that our conversation was over.

"Wait a minute Todd, we're not done yet. Please sit back down," Allen said. "You have worked wonders at the Eastern Plant, but there are still four other plants. And we have other 'old school' managers who still think the 'break it – fix it' mode of operation is acceptable. I need your help to implement changes throughout the company or we will run into the same type of problem that you experienced in the Eastern plant."

"Allen," I replied, "I'm fully prepared to take what we have developed, visit each site, and explain in detail what we developed and how we made it work. If you want, I am even more than willing to stay on at each site and help them make the change. With the outline and the change tools we have developed, we can achieve across the system what we achieved at the Eastern Plant."

"Not good enough, Todd," Allen responded with a hard look on his face. "If you think about it for a minute, what you are describing won't work. As you explained to me, you need a clear set of values and strong leadership to make a change of this significance. All you would be doing is trying to influence change but with no one expressly accountable to make it work over the long haul. You see, Todd, I was listening to all you said. I am firmly convinced that just a presentation accompanied by some coaching will fail. We need to drive the vision and the Goal Achievement Model and hold people accountable for the results.

"My idea for change is somewhat different. We need new leadership here at ATPCo. The managerial style of the managers at the various plants, excluding Pat of course, is counterproductive to what we are trying to achieve. There's a person who I would like you to meet. He will be joining us for lunch. His name is Mark Jones and he works at the Northern Plant. Mark is a lot like you. He knows what needs to be done and is willing to go head-to-head with management to make it happen — maybe not as forceful, but he also makes his point. The difference is Mark is production oriented.

"I believe that the two of you together can make an excellent team to help drive ATPCo to new and higher levels of performance. Therefore, I am going to create a matrix organization. You and Mark are going to work together. Mark will handle the production side of the business and you will handle the reliability and maintenance side. Effective immediately you both will become senior vice presidents reporting directly to me. The plant managers will no longer report to me; they will report to you and to Mark. Of course, this is going to be a major step change for them and many of the plant managers as well as their subordinates may have a problem with the organization I'm putting into place.

"I am making a firm commitment to you and Mark that if any, and I mean any of the managers can't or won't change, they will be relieved of their jobs. This is going to be our defining moment. Old school thinking dies here today. In addition, you will need to build a small staff of people who think like you do because there is a great deal of work ahead of us. Select who you want from anywhere in the company and let me have their names in a few weeks. They all will be reassigned to your team. I intend to make this work. The managers are not going to hold back the resources we need.

"Last, you will need to identify your replacement at the Eastern Plant. My only question is 'will you accept the job?' Oh, and one other thing. If you ever stop telling me what you actually believe to be in the best interests of the company — whether I like what you have to say or not — you will be fired. Agreed?"

Of course I agreed and I also accepted the job. During lunch Allen, Mark (who had flown in for a meeting with Allen the prior day), and I, discussed more details of our change strategy. Afterwards, I left the office floating on air. I had come a long way in a very short time, from practically being fired to vice president. Wasn't Doug going to be surprised (although I expected not for long) when he found out about his new reporting relationship? Wasn't Owen going to be surprised when he found out I had named him Eastern Plant Maintenance Manager? Wasn't the competition going to be surprised when they found out that they just could not compete with the new reliable ATP3Co.

I never did tell Allen about the e-mails. Change and improved reliability he could understand, but mystery e-mails guiding me through the change process was much more of a stretch. However, I had Allie's information regarding the e-mail source. I was determined to take a side trip to Blythe on the way home and drop in for a surprise visit to my mystery mentor. I owed him more than a simple thank you and wanted to deliver it in person.

It was only a short trip to Blythe. There was an airport right outside of town so I hired a private plane to take me there. Upon arrival, I rented a car and drove into town. Blythe looked just like the type of town you see in 1930s movies. Still, this was where Allie had told me the e-mails had originated. With her sources she had even provided me with an exact address.

The building wasn't large. It was a single-story building that looked like it hadn't been repainted or repaired for years. There was another larger office building on its left and a hardware store on the right. As I parked my car, I noticed activity in the larger building as well as the hardware store but no one entering or leaving the building I was about to visit, the identified home of my e-mail mentor. As I stepped through the door, I immediately understood why. The building was deserted.

So much for Allie's sources, I thought. After all of the time she spent and all of the money I had invested, all that I had as a result was an empty building in some back-water California town. Then I noticed that there was an office at the far end of the hall that had an open door and a light shining out into the hall. Maybe I wasn't at a dead end after all. It certainly couldn't hurt to look.

Walking up to the door and looking in, I was again disappointed. The office was empty. But then I noticed a brown manila envelope sitting on the desk with one word written in bold letters. The word was "Todd." To say I was astounded was an understatement. How could someone know I was going to come to this office on this day? That was my question and I knew in my heart it would never be answered. I was hoping, however, that the contents, whatever they might be, would give me some clue or insight to my mystery.

Opening the envelope was harder than I thought. My hands shook as I anticipated what I would find. Inside was a single piece of paper.

Todd,

Congratulations on your achievement! You have taken a major step towards helping to improve reliability and the overall profitability of ATPCo. I am sure you now realize that even though you led the effort (with some support) the real change was accomplished by those at the Eastern Plant. They were able to change their culture. They were able to move from a totally unsatisfactory way to conduct the work to a way that was far better. Now the equipment doesn't break down and if it does it is repaired in such a way as to never break in an unplanned fashion ever again.

Improving reliability is a difficult task. You must change the organization's culture and address the eight elements of change both individually and collectively. This change process can not be accomplished alone. And this is how I came into your life.

You asked me in many of your e-mails what you could do for me. I once asked that same question of the person who helped me turn my company from one of the worst in the industry to one of the best.

What my mentor told me at that time is exactly what I am going to tell you now. The way you can pay me back is by becoming one of us. There is a secret organization of people who have mentored others and helped them lead the effort to improve reliability of their companies. The members don't know one another and never reveal who they are to those they advise. The value is in the information itself, not in gaining recognition for providing it. The organization is simply called The Advisory Network or TAN.

If you choose to join, and I know you will, all you need to do is to provide the information you have learned to someone else who desperately needs it in the same way you needed it when you arrived at the Eastern Plant. His name is Art Stewart and his e-mail address is AStewart@SGT.com. He is a maintenance manager like you were and works for SGT Industries. Todd, Art is in trouble.

Welcome to TAN and good luck.

EPILOGUE

Art Stewart had an incredibly frustrating day. The production line went down once again and his manager called him every name in the book, even some he had never heard before. It was bad enough that the main pump failed, causing a line shutdown that would take days to correct. But worse, the same pump had failed just one week earlier for the same reason. Art knew there had to be a better way to run the plant, a way in which equipment didn't unexpectedly fail. He and his machinery engineers should be able to recognize failure as it was developing, not just after it had happened. Art truly believed that if he had been 55, he would have retired on the spot rather than continue working in this non-productive manner. But he wasn't 55 and instead had many years remaining in his career.

Sitting at his desk, he pulled up his e-mail account to see what other unplanned disasters had happened that would add even more distress to the day. The e-mail on the screen confused Art. It was addressed to him but from someone he did not know — a totally unrecognizable name. It read simply:

```
From: TAN
To: Art Stewart

Reliability is the key to your
salvation.
```

Art Stewart's journey to improved reliability and my role in The Advisory Network had begun.

To all those working in a world like mine had been, remember:

Reliability is the key to your salvation.
Todd Bradley (TAN)

<u>Summary Data</u>
(from individual element questions)

	Max	Score
Leadership	20	
Work Process	20	
Structure	20	
Group Learning	20	
Technology	20	
Communication	20	
Interrelationships	20	
Rewards	20	

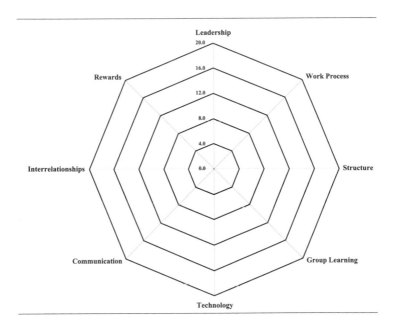

A. Leadership	Points	Score

1		
Rate the reaction of the site personnel to the leadership of the plant.		
A. High level of effort to follow the leaders	4	
B. Average level of effort to follow the leaders	3	
C. Minimal effort	2	
D. The organization does not support the leaders	1	
E. There is outright resistance to the leadership	0	

2		
The leadership is focused on leading the organization towards a vision of the future. While they are concerned with the activities of the day this is not their primary focus.		
A. Strongly agree	4	
B. Agree	3	
C. Neutral	2	
D. Disagree	1	
E. Strongly disagree	0	

3		
Management allows the organization freedom to act within a set of predefined boundaries without micromanaging of its efforts.		
A. Strongly agree	4	
B. Agree	3	
C. Neutral	2	
D. Disagree	1	
E. Strongly disagree	0	

4		
When the organization develops and implements goals, initiatives, and activities, those involved are held accountable for success.		
A. Strongly agree	4	
B. Agree	3	
C. Neutral	2	
D. Disagree	1	
E. Strongly disagree	0	

5		
The leader's (at all levels) words about improving are "clearly" supported by their actions. In other words they "walk the talk."		
A. Strongly agree	4	
B. Agree	3	
C. Neutral	2	
D. Disagree	1	
E. Strongly disagree	0	

A. Leadership		
	vs. a maximum score of...	20

B. Work Process	Points	Score

1			
Work processes have been developed focused on achieving the vision and are in use at the work site.			
A. Strongly agree	4		
B. Agree	3		
C. Neutral	2		
D. Disagree	1		
E. Strongly disagree	0		

2			
The work processes are reviewed and updated as improvements are made or as new and improved ways of doing business are learned.			
A. Strongly agree	4		
B. Agree	3		
C. Neutral	2		
D. Disagree	1		
E. Strongly disagree	0		

3			
Measurements are in place to determine if the processes are working properly. Corrective action is taken if they are not.			
A. Strongly agree	4		
B. Agree	3		
C. Neutral	2		
D. Disagree	1		
E. Strongly disagree	0		

4			
The processes were designed to represent a desired future state so that the site can use them as a goals for achieving excellence.			
A. Strongly agree	4		
B. Agree	3		
C. Neutral	2		
D. Disagree	1		
E. Strongly disagree	0		

5			
The processes were developed by a team whose goal was to improve how work is accomplished.			
A. Strongly agree	4		
B. Agree	3		
C. Neutral	2		
D. Disagree	1		
E. Strongly disagree	0		

B. Work Process		
vs. a maximum score of...		20

C. Structure	Points		Score

1		
The organization's structure supports the business vision and strategy to achieve it.		
A. Strongly agree	4	
B. Agree	3	
C. Neutral	2	
D. Disagree	1	
E. Strongly disagree	0	

2		
The structure supports the work processes within a department and between departments (across the departmental interfaces).		
A. Strongly agree	4	
B. Agree	3	
C. Neutral	2	
D. Disagree	1	
E. Strongly disagree	0	

3		
The structure supports people working together in teams to accomplish the business objectives.		
A. Strongly agree	4	
B. Agree	3	
C. Neutral	2	
D. Disagree	1	
E. Strongly disagree	0	

4		
The structure was designed to support communications and interrelationships both internally (within a department) and externally (between departments).		
A. Strongly agree	4	
B. Agree	3	
C. Neutral	2	
D. Disagree	1	
E. Strongly disagree	0	

5		
The levels in the structure from the bottom of the organization (the workforce) to the top (the manager of the plant or facility) appears to be correct in that they support effective execution of the work.		
A. Strongly agree	4	
B. Agree	3	
C. Neutral	2	
D. Disagree	1	
E. Strongly disagree	0	

C. Structure		
vs. a maximum score of...		20

D. Group Learning	Points	Score

1

Rate the level of management support for learning new, different and better ways of working within the organization.

A. Very supportive (an integral part of the work effort)	4
B. Supportive	3
C. Neutral	2
D. Non supportive	1
E. It is not present at the site	0

2

The personnel in the organization are allotted time for learning and training each year (excluding mandatory training) and are encouraged to use the time.

A. Strongly agree	4
B. Agree	3
C. Neutral	2
D. Disagree	1
E. Strongly disagree	0

3

Training and group learning are not aimed just at job performance skills, but also skills that promote better interaction and teamwork.

A. Strongly agree	4
B. Agree	3
C. Neutral	2
D. Disagree	1
E. Strongly disagree	0

4

When training is to be developed, an effort is made to determine the difference between what employees already know and what they need to know.

A. Strongly agree	4
B. Agree	3
C. Neutral	2
D. Disagree	1
E. Strongly disagree	0

5

Employees have input into what they are going to learn.

A. Strongly agree	4
B. Agree	3
C. Neutral	2
D. Disagree	1
E. Strongly disagree	0

D. Group Learning	
vs. a maximum score of...	**20**

E. Technology	Points	Score

1

Software tools that support the work process exist and are well utilized.

A. Strongly agree	4
B. Agree	3
C. Neutral	2
D. Disagree	1
E. Strongly disagree	0

2

The software is integrated into a single electronic system in order to simplify use and avoid multiple entries and databases that could cause problems.

A. Strongly agree	4
B. Agree	3
C. Neutral	2
D. Disagree	1
E. Strongly disagree	0

3

The data within the system is easily accessible to all employees who need it.

A. Strongly agree	4
B. Agree	3
C. Neutral	2
D. Disagree	1
E. Strongly disagree	0

4

The plant has a strategic multiyear plan for enhancing software in order to stay current with the technology and to provide high levels of support to the workforce.

A. Strongly agree	4
B. Agree	3
C. Neutral	2
D. Disagree	1
E. Strongly disagree	0

5

Support that is readily available for both the users and the system exists at the site.

A. Strongly agree	4
B. Agree	3
C. Neutral	2
D. Disagree	1
E. Strongly disagree	0

E. Technology	
vs. a maximum score of...	20

F. Communication	Points	Score

1

The leaders of the organization (at the site level) believe that communication is important and visibly practice what they believe.

A. Strongly agree	4
B. Agree	3
C. Neutral	2
D. Disagree	1
E. Strongly disagree	0

2

All other levels of the organization also believe in the importance of good communication and demonstrate this belief at all times.

A. Strongly agree	4
B. Agree	3
C. Neutral	2
D. Disagree	1
E. Strongly disagree	0

3

Events that occur at the site are well communicated so that employees are aware of what is going on.

A. Strongly agree	4
B. Agree	3
C. Neutral	2
D. Disagree	1
E. Strongly disagree	0

4

Meetings include: an agenda, a pre-established start and stop time, facilitation, and minutes, with action items, of what was discussed.

A. Strongly agree	4
B. Agree	3
C. Neutral	2
D. Disagree	1
E. Strongly disagree	0

5

Communication tools (intranet, voice mail, e-mail, phones and radios) are provided to those who need them and are effectively utilized.

A. Strongly agree	4
B. Agree	3
C. Neutral	2
D. Disagree	1
E. Strongly disagree	0

F. Communication	
vs. a maximum score of...	20

G. Interrelationships

		Points	Score

1

The top to bottom working relationship within the organization is mature and supports change initiatives.

	Points	Score
A. Strongly agree	4	
B. Agree	3	
C. Neutral	2	
D. Disagree	1	
E. Strongly disagree	0	

2

The working relationship among peers and across departments is mature enough to support change initiatives.

	Points	Score
A. Strongly agree	4	
B. Agree	3	
C. Neutral	2	
D. Disagree	1	
E. Strongly disagree	0	

3

When teams are formed to work on projects (including implementation of change) the relationships are well developed and mutually supportive.

	Points	Score
A. Strongly agree	4	
B. Agree	3	
C. Neutral	2	
D. Disagree	1	
E. Strongly disagree	0	

4

The working relationship between the workforce (union or nonunion) and management is supportive of change initiatives.

	Points	Score
A. Strongly agree	4	
B. Agree	3	
C. Neutral	2	
D. Disagree	1	
E. Strongly disagree	0	

5

The working relationship between the various locations (e.g. corporate headquarters and plant sites) is mature to the point that best work practices are shared and used.

	Points	Score
A. Strongly agree	4	
B. Agree	3	
C. Neutral	2	
D. Disagree	1	
E. Strongly disagree	0	

G. Interrelationships

	Score
vs. a maximum score of...	20

H. Rewards	Points		Score

1

People recognize that rewards are not always in the form of personal financial gain but can be attained through business success for the team.

	Points
A. Strongly agree	4
B. Agree	3
C. Neutral	2
D. Disagree	1
E. Strongly disagree	0

2

There is a viable process in place to provide short-term rewards to reinforce change efforts by the organization.

	Points
A. Strongly agree	4
B. Agree	3
C. Neutral	2
D. Disagree	1
E. Strongly disagree	0

3

All reward plans require input comes from managers, subordinates, and peers evaluating how the individual performed both individually and as a team member.

	Points
A. Strongly agree	4
B. Agree	3
C. Neutral	2
D. Disagree	1
E. Strongly disagree	0

4

A process exists that addresses longer term rewards for those who actively support change (i.e. promotion, change focused work assignments)

	Points
A. Strongly agree	4
B. Agree	3
C. Neutral	2
D. Disagree	1
E. Strongly disagree	0

5

The financial success of the business is shared through a gain or profit sharing plan with those who contributed.

	Points
A. Excellent	4
B. Good	3
C. Average	2
E. Very Poor	0

H. Rewards		
vs. a maximum score of...		**20**

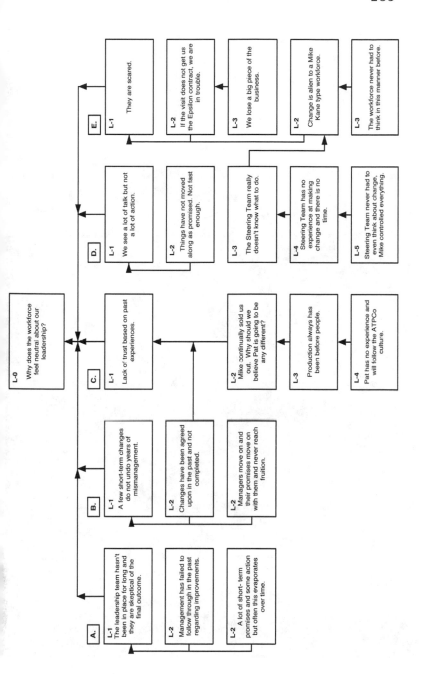

AND THE JOURNEY
CONTINUES...